SUZY PRUDDEN'S FAMILY FITNESS BOOK

Also by Suzy Prudden and Jeffrey Sussman:
Suzy Prudden's Creative Fitness for Baby and Child

SUZY PRUDDEN'S

FAMILY FITNESS BOOK

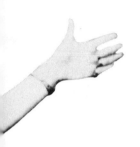

SUZY PRUDDEN AND JEFFREY SUSSMAN

Photographs by Jeffrey Sussman

Publishers • GROSSET & DUNLAP • New York
A FILMWAYS COMPANY

To the families who were
For the family who is

Published simultaneously in Canada
Library of Congress catalog card number: 75-11883
ISBN: 0-448-14502-2
First paperback edition 1978
Printed in the United States of America

The author wishes to thank Dr. Jean Mayer for permission to quote excerpts
from *Overweight Causes, Costs and Control,* copyright © 1968, Prentice-Hall,
Englewood Cliffs, New Jersey.

CONTENTS

PREFACE

MY WORLD AND WELCOME TO IT

Chickens get up before I do, only because I am not as plucky.

I do not spring from wheat-germ dreams into deep-knee bends. Yet, I am healthy, energetic, and eager to welcome each day. My husband, Jeffrey, and my son, Robby, are much the same way.

Robby rises with the sun, then he clicks on his television. Jeffrey often writes into the quiet of midnight and any attempt to wake him the next morning is like a kick to the Rock of Gibraltar. Something finally rouses him, though, and we all have a healthful breakfast.

Of course, I settle for the lightest foods, for I feel the heaviest. I have a few favorite diets. And each lets me down gently.

After our Airedale has been walked, we three leave for the day. I head for my studio, while Jeffrey walks Robby ten blocks to school. Afterward, Jeffrey comes to the studio. We go through the mail and discuss the day's business.

As soon as he leaves, I start my first class, continuing until lunch. Occasionally a business meeting, a lecture, or a television appearance drags me from my studio, but I have a well-trained staff, quick to step in when I step out.

After a model's lunch I dash to my East Side studio. At three o'clock I begin a few hours of private classes for adults and/or children with special problems. Most often, they have been referred by physicians.

At about the same time, my son dives into a swimming lesson, or jumps into an exercise class, or concentrates on a paintbrush, or lets his fingers do the walking on a keyboard.

In the evening, we like to enjoy one another: games, stories, television, or a night out. On Saturday morning, I have to be in a television studio by 7:00 AM; I am usually finished by noon, so if the weather is wintry, we take to the mountains. Skiing and sleighing are great relaxercisers. Now and then, I am served breakfast in bed on Sunday; small favors are greatly appreciated, even when I'm on a diet.

During the summer, we run a recreational program in Bridgehampton, Long Island. Horseback riding, tennis, swimming, rowing, and a variety of games and sports are all part of our summer fun.

Indeed, we are a busy family. Not only busy, but close and happy, too. We are a family on the go, a family having a good time together.

Every family can and should be physically fit. Physical fitness is not only a foundation for a successful life, it is an essential ingredient. I wish to share physical fitness with you. What follows is not merely instructive, it is meant to be fun for your entire family. Because the book deals specifically with a variety of sports and activities, exercises are repeated in full for the convenience of the reader.

I hope to add not only excitement to your lives, but health and longevity, too.

INTRODUCTION

ALL IN THE FITNESS FAMILY

No one enjoys exercising alone. It is boring, if not tedious. Yet, no one alive can hope to possess a better health-insurance policy than a program for physical fitness. I advocate neither military calisthenics nor spartan regimens, but suggest a few enjoyable hours of exercise every week. Scientifically, no more is required for a fit body. The entire family should participate, for it strengthens family bonds as well as bodies. In addition, what parent does not want healthy, physically fit children? In fact, what parent does not want to inhabit a healthy, physically fit body?

A healthy family is a healthy unit, able to enjoy life, able to enjoy themselves, together and as individuals.

WHAT IS THE PHYSICALLY FIT FAMILY?

The Physically Fit Family is one for whom weekends are not the tag ends of exhausting weekdays. The physically fit family is healthy, vigorous, and vivacious. They want to live long, exciting lives. They do what's best for their children, from infancy upward. They participate in numerous activities: jogging, bicycling, tennis, skiing, climbing, swimming—the list is nearly infinite. And so are life's pleasures.

They know physical fitness means a strong heart, healthy brain cells, and energy and strength to tackle success. Their diets are well planned. Their bloodstreams are not polluted by too much sugar.

Why Should a Family Be Physically Fit?

Technology (as beneficial as it is) has made passivity the way to a non-life. With the push of a button, the pull of a lever, the press of a pedal, one can accomplish nearly anything. By pulling one's own levers—muscles—one can reach great physical realms.

The President's Council on Physical Fitness issued the following statement: "There is strong authoritative support for the concept that regular exercise can prevent degenerative diseases and slow down the physical deterioration that accompanies aging." And as Hans Kraus, M.D., wrote in the foreword of my book *Creative Fitness for Baby and Child:* ". . . the medical profession has been increasingly aware of the importance of exercise to correct the noxious influence of our sedentary, mechanized, overstressed way of life."

My grandfather walked at least five miles per day; he lived into his ninety-sixth year. And of course he was an example for all.

But each individual in my family has been following, thus setting, examples not only for physical fitness, but for family togetherness as well.

When my father rock-climbed, I might have snapped his picture. But I have a more reliable record: I climbed with him. And a healthy body is worth a thousand pictures of healthful activity.

When my mother skied, I could have warmed myself with a hot-buttered rum. But the warmth of our affection, racing down a slope, was a far better run for my money.

In particular, exercise provides physical endurance, and that endurance is like fuel in the body's engines.

Without exercise, fatigue, like an overheated engine, grinds you to a halt.

Without exercise, your nerves may become frazzled, sparking explosions of temper.

Without a well-tuned engine, the heat of stress and tension may leave you where neither body shop nor body builder can get you running again.

Where to begin? In the crib. In physical fitness, the maxim "better late than never" does not always apply. If you wait too long, the strain might be too great. The fitness habit begun in infancy is a solid foundation for a constructive lifetime. Remember: 50 percent of a child's physical potential is developed by age four!

And as a child grows, fitness means energy for school work, strength for competition, and an attractive, healthy body. Without a strong, healthy body a child lacks the self-confidence for all future activities.

Through the middle years, physical fitness helps keep us young. Furthermore, that great bane of middle age, the heart attack, can frequently be avoided by maintaining a fit body. For the older person, physical fitness means living on your own power. Not leaning on the strength of another.

A body should be as finely tuned as a Rolls-Royce; keep it so, and it will run smoothly and efficiently to all life's destinations.

1

In the Beginning: The Couple

There are innumerable reasons why individuals marry. I shall deal with only one of those reasons: the physical.

Even animals in the wild evaluate prospective mates. A lion will reject a lioness if the latter is unable to hunt. Of course, human evaluations are far more subtle and complete. You naturally want your mate to be intelligent and capable of managing responsibilities, but the first eye-catcher is the physique—a signal of health and well-being to anyone with sensitive antennae.

There is no question: most of us respond to attractive people. And attractive people tend to have firm, well-exercised bodies.

The Importance of a Flat Stomach

Ah, those stomachs. Too often they seem to bulge or sag in a variety of sad and comical shapes. I make light of it, but not because I lack sympathy. I had a big belly at one time, too. It made life difficult, so I have trimmed away that fat.

A big, soft belly is like an overstuffed sofa. Such a stomach not only indicates a superfluous diet, but a dearth of exercise as well. And its owner may prove an inadequate lover, for sex requires strength. Specifically, a big belly encumbers the movements of bones and muscles necessary to a satisfying sex life.

If a stomach balloons or slopes, it's because of weak stomach muscles. In *Your Heart and How to Live with It*, Dr. Lawrence E. Lamb wrote: "If you pick up the skin on the abdomen, around the umbilicus, and flatten the fold of skin out and it is over a half inch thick, there is too much fat present."

When stomach muscles are out of work and not supporting the family of abdominal organs, then other muscles must work overtime. Back muscles are forced to do the abdominals' work, and pay is not time and a half—it is a backache. Soon the body begins to suffer poor posture, putting stress on other muscles. Serious as such a condition is, it may be corrected by simple exercises and intelligent dieting.

Even more alarming is what happens to the heart and arteries. If the belly is big, then the fatty deposits in arteries are at a dangerously high level. These fatty deposits are commonly known as cholesterol. If nothing is done about cholesterol, if the condition remains and hardens, then arteriosclerosis occurs. So if there is someone you love (even yourself), motivate him toward a life of physical fitness.

A Hard Bottom Means a Strong Marriage

Buttocks that jiggle when you walk inspire a laugh; but they, in fact, often portend a less than active sex life.

Anyone who spends eight or more hours sitting is hardly exercising. In fact, one's gluteus maximus will seem to exceed normal maximum proportions. Yet there are several simple, even surreptitious, exercises to do, and I shall describe them in the section concluding this chapter.

The Heart of the Matter

As I wrote in the stomach section, arteriosclerosis often results from improper dieting and insufficient exercise.

Doctors have learned that more people suffer from this condition in America than in less affluent nations. One reason: Our diets are rich in unhealthful foods; another: Modern technology permits us not to exercise.

I must again quote Dr. Lawrence E. Lamb: "Several benefits can be expected from a successful exercise program. There is an improvement in the blood flow to your heart muscle. The development of additional blood supply and the development of connections between the different arteries significantly improves the likelihood that an occlusion of any one vessel will not produce major damage to your heart muscle. It can't provide a guarantee but it will improve your chances. In this sense, it serves as an insurance policy."

And now quoting my mother, Bonnie Prudden: "If you exercise regularly you can control obesity, a prime factor in heart disease and many other diseases as well. Exercise burns up fat that would otherwise be stored to your detriment."

Remember: Your heart is the most important muscle in your body. Ignore it, and it will cease to function.

LIFE AND BREATH

Earlier, I wrote of cholesterol: a fatlike substance that acts as a dam in blood vessels. If arteries leading to and from the heart have too much cholesterol, then the heart will have difficulty pumping.

If you suffer such a problem, and then puff a noxious cigarette, you may induce a chronic lung ailment.

Such suffering lungs may be unable to provide adequate oxygen to the blood. This means the oxidized blood needed for exertion is curtailed, and the heart must work harder than it should.

So if a flight of stairs makes you huff and puff like a rusty locomotive, you're on the wrong track.

If a sprint for a bus leaves you breathless as well as busless, you are on the platform of physical non-fitness.

LOVE ME, NOT MY FAT

Cyril Connolly, the British critic, wrote: "Imprisoned in every fat man, a thin one is wildly signalling to be let out."

Yet, when you are fat, all eyes see a fat person—hardly an imprisoned thin one.

Fat cannot be tossed aside as easily as last year's styles. Fat must be worked off. Your thin prisoner must command you to exercise, to diet. It will not be easy, but the battles worth fighting never are. If they were, they would not be great battles.

To begin, you must:

THINK THIN; THINK BEAUTIFUL

I am not referring to mere daydreaming; rather, I mean what is commonly known as "positive thinking." As an actor and actress think their ways into roles, you must think your way out of those rolls of fat. If you are going to be thin and physically fit, then you must believe it, think it.

Once you have begun to think thin, then you will diet and exercise. Within days, you will begin to feel proud of your new body. The greater your pride, the greater your efforts. Finally, you will be what you have always wanted to be—slim and attractive.

Remember: Every pound of fat can be converted to five pounds of muscle, which occupies a lot less space. Well-exercised muscles are not only compact, they are elegant. You will not only be thinner, you will be more energetic, more exciting, and better company than your previous self. Not only you, but your lover, too, will love you for your efforts.

So set your mind on the track to thinness; it is not a distant journey.

SEXERCISES

Making love with a soft, fat body is not as stimulating or fulfilling as making love with a firm, slender one. Flexibility and muscle control play an important role in lovemaking. Through exercise, the body can receive and give pleasure never thought possible. I hope to show you how you can build a flexible body so that you may enjoy sex to its fullest. To keep a beautiful and fit body one should exercise 30 to 40 minutes a day. Incorporate the following exercises into your daily exercise routine.

The pelvic area could not be more important. Good stomach and lower back muscles are essential for lovemaking. They are not the only muscles needed, but they are the basic ones. Flexibility is extremely important; endurance is essential.

In order to control the pelvic area, you must learn to isolate it from the rest of your body. This sounds difficult, but after a little practice it is really quite simple.

1. HIP WAG

Stand with feet apart and arms slightly raised at your sides. Push your hip to the right, leaning most of your weight on the right leg. Now change direction, pushing your hip to the left, leaning most of your weight on the left leg. (Be sure not to stick your buttocks out.) Keep wagging your hips from right to left, keeping the upper half of your body still. Repeat 20 times.

1

2. PELVIC AREA—TIGHTEN/RELEASE

Stand with feet together. Pull your stomach in, tighten your buttocks (and for women, simultaneously, the inner vaginal muscles), hold for 4 seconds, and release. Repeat up to 16 times. This may be done while walking (walk 4 steps while tightening muscles, then release for 4 steps), standing in a room, or even while window-shopping. You can even sit at a desk and do this exercise while working.

3. PELVIC TILT

Being a passive lover is no fun for your partner. In order for both of you to get the most pleasure out of lovemaking you must use the motion of the pelvic area to enhance the pleasure from the motion of the genital area.

a. Stand with feet apart and knees bent. Place hands on thighs. Without moving legs or upper back and shoulders, stick buttocks out. Now (as if someone came up behind you and slapped your fanny) tuck buttocks under and tighten stomach muscles quickly. Stick buttocks out again, but do *not* move your legs, upper back, or shoulders. Repeat 8 to 16 times.

2

3

b. Lie supine with knees bent. Arch lower back, keeping buttocks and upper back on the floor. Now tuck pelvis under so that your entire

4

back is flat on the floor, and the lower half of your buttocks is off the floor. Keep the movements smooth and the motion at an even tempo. If counting helps, count: push out, 1—2; tuck under, 1—2. Repeat 8 times.

4. SIT-UPS—GRABBING KNEES

Now for the all-important stomach muscles.

Lie supine, legs out straight, and put arms straight out above head. Now swing arms over head and bring body to a sitting position, at the same time bending knees so that you can grab your knees with your hands. Now tighten stomach, and push forward with the small of your back, until you are sitting with a straight back. Hold this position (keeping stomach muscles tight) for 4 seconds, then release and return to original supine position. Repeat 8 times.

If this tires you out or makes you ache, do only 4 to start and gradually work up to 8.

8

5. ON BACK—HIP LIFT

Lie supine with arms flat at sides, feet apart, and knees bent. Now lift your buttocks off the floor, pushing hips toward the ceiling. Hold 4 seconds and return to resting position. Repeat 8 times.

6. HIP LIFT

For greater movability in pelvic area.

Stand with feet slightly apart and hands at sides. Keep shoulders still. Now lift the right hip up and slightly forward, lifting the right heel and turning the hip inward as if you wanted to see something on the right side of your buttocks. Return to starting position and repeat 4 times. Now do the same with your left hip, repeating 4 times. Do series twice.

9

7. PELVIC CIRCLE

Have you ever watched children with a Hula-Hoop? Their pelvic area seems to turn as the hoop spins. It looks impossible, but it is really quite simple. The most important thing to remember is to keep your pelvic area isolated from the rest of your body.

Stand with feet slightly apart and knees slightly bent. Stick the right hip out (as in no. 1, HIP WAG), now arch lower back, pushing buttocks out (as in no. 2, PELVIC TILT). Now stick the left hip out and then tuck your pelvis under (as in no. 3, PELVIC TILT). Your pelvic area should make a full circle, but the rest of your body should remain stationary. Start slowly until you find the going easy, and then pick up the pace, keeping the movements smooth. Repeat pelvic circle 16 times. Change direction after 8.

11

10

13

12

8. PELVIC TILT, KNEELING

Kneel with legs slightly apart. Keep shoulders still and buttocks *off* your calves. Keep upper body still and stick your fanny out. Now tuck your fanny under (contracting stomach muscles). Repeat 16 times.

9. PELVIC CIRCLE, KNEELING

Do the same exercise you did for PELVIC CIRCLE, no. 7, only do this exercise on your knees, beginning in the same position as for PELVIC TILT, KNEELING, no. 8. Do 16 times.

10. PRONE LEG LIFT

This exercise is excellent for the lower back muscles. It is extremely important for men as they use their lower-back muscles for longer periods of time during lovemaking than do women. It would not only be awkward, but extremely disappointing if one's lower back went into spasm in the middle of lovemaking.

Lie on your stomach, resting your head on folded arms. Keep legs straight and hipbones on the floor. Alternate lifting first one leg (hold 4 seconds), then the other leg (hold 4 seconds). Repeat 12 times.

11. WEIGHTED PRONE LEG LIFTS

After exercise no. 10 becomes quite easy, strap on 2 lb. ankle weights and repeat exercise 12 times. Men should work their way to 5 lbs.; women should keep the weight at 2 lbs. If you find your lower back aching—return to the exercise without weights.

12. PRONE LEG LIFTS OVER BACK
TO TOUCH OPPOSITE HAND

This may look impossible, but as you gain in strength and flexibility, it is quite simple. Do not do this exercise for the first few weeks.

Lie prone with legs straight, feet apart, and hands at sides, about a foot from your body. Lift your left leg and hip off the floor, bend knee, and cross the leg over your buttocks until your toes touch your right

17

18

19

hand. Then return to starting position. Now do the same with your right leg, crossing over to touch your left hand. Repeat each leg lift 4 times.

13. BE A TABLE

Terrific for arm and leg strength as well as upper and lower back.

Sit on the floor with feet apart and knees bent. Place hands slightly to the side and behind you. Now lift buttocks off the floor, raising stomach into the air. You should form a square with the floor as your base. Hold body in this position 4 seconds, then return to starting position. Repeat 6 times.

20

14. ON TABLE LEG LIFTS

As in no. 10, this exercise is for your lower back.

Lie prone across a table, letting legs hang down to the floor from

21

22

your hips. Now lift both legs into the air so that your legs straighten and incline slightly upward. Hold legs in this position 4 seconds. Now return to the relaxed position. Repeat 6 times.

FLEXIBILITY

15. FORWARD BOUNCE (SITTING)

Sit on the floor. Put one sole of your foot against the other sole. Of course your knees will be bent and apart. Grasp ankles and, keeping back straight, rock your torso forward and back 6 times. Now round your back, and pull your head toward your toes and bounce 6 times. Repeat series 4 times.

16. KNEES TO FLOOR

This is especially good for stretching the inner leg muscles.

Seated with the soles of your feet together and knees apart, place your hands on your ankles, and your elbows on your knees. Push your knees toward the floor with your elbows, as far as you can, then release. (Do not push to the point of pain. Just go as far as your muscles will allow.) Repeat 12 times.

23

24

17. LEGS STRAIGHT FORWARD BOUNCE

This exercise is excellent for back stretch and leg flexibility.

On the floor, sit with legs straight in front of you and feet together; toes pointed. Grab lower calves, and keeping knees straight, bounce forward 8 times. Now flex feet and bounce forward 8 times. Repeat series twice.

18. SIDE TO SIDE BOUNCES

This exercise will not only stretch the backs and insides of your legs, it will help stretch back and upper hip areas.

a. Sit with legs wide apart and straight. Hold right knee, flex foot to give the backs of your leg muscles and tendons greater stretching, and keep head up. Now push torso forward and back. Try to feel as if you were stretching your chin toward your toes. After 8 bounces, change legs. Remember: Keep your chin up.

25

26

b. Sit as in 18*a*, only this time try to pull your ear to your knee without bending the knee. Bounce 8 times and change legs.

Do series *a* and *b* 3 times.

19. LEGS OVERHEAD BACK STRETCH

Lie supine. Bring your knees over your chest. Slowly straighten your legs vertically. When your legs are straight, start to lift your buttocks off the floor while lowering your legs over your head. Try to get your feet on the floor above your head, but don't force them. Go as far as you can and hold 4 seconds. Then return to supine position, bending your knees as you lower your legs. Repeat 4 times.

27

20. ONE LEG STRETCH

a. Lie on your left side, leaning on your left forearm. Bend left leg at the knee. Bring right leg up and with the right hand grab it by the calf. Now straighten right leg up into the air and pull straight right leg toward right shoulder 4 times and then release. Repeat 4 times and change sides.

28

29

b. After several weeks, as *a* becomes easy, change exercise slightly. Lie on floor as in *a*. Grab the inside of your right foot and straighten right leg. As in *a*, pull leg toward your shoulder. Pull 4 times and release. Repeat 4 times and change sides.

30

31

Endurance

Lovemaking is not just a shot in the dark. The longer you spend at it, the more pleasurable it is. To be a good lover, you need endurance.

21. RUN IN PLACE

Run in place for 5 minutes each day. After a few weeks, make it 10 minutes. Work your way up to 15 minutes. Be sure to start slowly, and if you feel too tired, STOP. Run again later.

22. JUMP ROPE

Start with 10 jumps. Each week add 5 more jumps, until you reach 50. If you feel out of breath after 10 or 15 jumps, STOP. Do a different exercise, and then do another 15 jumps.

23. PUSH-UPS

This exercise is not only good for endurance, it is excellent for upper back, chest, and shoulder strength. It builds beautiful pectoral muscles on men and helps firm sagging breasts on women.

Start from the top.

Many people are not strong enough to do a push-up properly. Rather than struggle and end up doing it incorrectly, possibly hurting yourself, make it a little easier.

Get in a push-up position resting on your hands and the balls of your feet (as if you had just raised your body from the floor). Keep your body straight, then slowly lower yourself to the floor—put your chest on the floor FIRST. Then relax. Get up easily and repeat, going down slowly. Count to 4 while lowering yourself. Repeat 4 times. When this becomes easy, try a regular push-up. Starting from the floor, keeping your body straight, raise yourself up until your arms are straight. Then slowly lower yourself. Do as many as you can. Start with 3 and work up to 20 or 25. If you can do 50 CORRECTLY, that's terrific!

2

THE CRADLE ROCKS

Having a baby can and should be a joyous, creative experience. But a woman must be trained for such labor.

For too many, post-pregnancy leaves the new mother limp and out of shape. That does not have to be the case. If a fighter trains for a match, then why not a woman getting ready for delivery? Since the baby is stretching her stomach muscles, pushing around her internal organs, and putting a strain on her heart and her circulation, shouldn't she be working toward peak condition?

During and after pregnancy, strong, flexible muscles are of prime importance. They not only hold you in, they assist your maneuverings: At least 50 percent of America's women are not in good condition for a pregnancy. Many make their lives difficult by adding too much weight. And that weight is not only difficult to lose after giving birth; it can be dangerous during pregnancy when your heart is already under increased pressure.

During pregnancy, an out-of-shape physique causes back and leg aches, making feet feel heavy. With all those aches, the pregnant woman usually attempts to rest. Then she gets up and eats. The unhealthful pattern goes on—unless, of course, she has the courage to break the spell.

I exercised up to my ninth month. That is not advised for everyone—you should consult your physician before you commence with my program. But I had a wonderful time and was active and enthusiastic throughout.

Obviously, exercise is not only beneficial, it is essential. It helps to keep your heart strong and your body unencumbered by too much fat. And if you follow my special exercises, under your physician's guidance, you will probably keep your weight down and your health and spirits high. Remember: Eat healthful foods; exercise away superfluous calories.

Well-exercised abdominal muscles, though stretched during pregnancy, may be tightened by a few minutes of exercise every day after recovery. My special exercises are not only formulated to tighten those stretched muscles, but to strengthen others as well. Strong abdominals will keep the organs of the abdominal cavity in place. Strong pectoral muscles will support breasts. And my special exercises can even trim waists and thin thighs, making one lithe and lovely, feminine and ready to feel maternal.

So even if you were not in the best of shape before, I shall help you tailor a new and better shape now.

Bras and girdles are merely substitutes for muscles—they lack the functional elegance of a well-toned body. Once you have strong, flexible muscles, you will be self-admiring as well as admired.

PREGNANCY EXERCISES

Staying healthy and strong during pregnancy requires careful attention. The proper food is essential for the proper growth of the fetus; the proper exercise is essential for the well-being of the new mother. Without the adequate muscle strength, women become more frequently overfatigued and tense than those who exercise regularly. Keeping in shape during pregnancy permits a woman to regain a beautiful figure after baby is born.

Check with your doctor; show him the list of exercises in this chapter. He will tell you which ones are good for you (not every exercise is for everyone). To keep in shape try to exercise 15 to 20 minutes a day.

1. SIT-UPS

Sit on the floor with legs straight, placing feet under something sturdy whenever possible. Place hands behind neck. Slowly lie down to a supine position; then, keeping hands behind neck, sit up. Start with 5 and work your way up to 20, adding a few more each week.

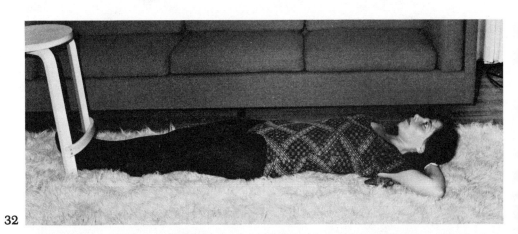

32

33

34

2. BACK ARCH AND FLATTEN

Lie supine with knees bent and feet on floor. Keeping your upper back and buttocks on the floor, arch your lower back. Now flatten it, pushing it onto the floor. Hold your back firmly against the floor for 4 seconds and repeat the arch-and-flattening process. Repeat 6 times.

3. FLAT BACK—LEG LOWER

This exercise is essential for lower-back strength. Remember, as the weight of your baby increases, the strain on your lower-back muscles increases, too.

Lie supine. Bring knees over chest and then straighten legs so they form a 90-degree angle with your torso. Keeping the small of your back pressed against the floor, slowly lower legs. Lower them ONLY as far as you can WITHOUT your back rising off the floor. (If you feel your back rising, you have lowered your legs too far.) When you reach *your* point, hold 4 seconds, then release by bending your knees over your chest. Repeat 4 times. NEVER lower your legs all the way down to the floor as this will cause back strain. Be sure to go only as far as you can, keeping your back FLAT.

37

38

39

4. FORWARD BOUNCE (SITTING)

Sit on the floor. Put one sole of your foot against the other sole. Of course your knees will be bent and apart. Grasp ankles and, keeping back straight, rock your torso forward and back 6 times. Now round your back, and pull your head toward your toes and bounce 6 times. Repeat series 4 times.

5. KNEES TO FLOOR

This is especially good for stretching the inner leg muscles.

Seated with the soles of your feet together and knees apart, place your hands on your ankles, and your elbows on your knees. Push your knees toward the floor with your elbows, as far as you can, then release. (Do not push to the point of pain. Just go as far as your muscles will allow.) Repeat 12 times.

6. ON ELBOWS BICYCLE

Good for stomach and lower-back strength.

Sitting on the floor, lean on elbows and forearms. Pretend you are pedaling a bike. As you bring your right knee up to your chest, straighten left leg (but don't rest it on the floor). Now bring your left leg up and straighten the right one. Get a smooth circular motion going. Do 16.

7. ON ELBOWS, KNEES TO CHEST,
STRAIGHTEN, AND CIRCLE

This is a very difficult exercise and requires strong stomach muscles. If you are new to exercise, wait a few weeks before adding this one to your daily program.

41

Lean back on elbows as in no. 6. Bend both knees up to chest. Straighten legs up in the air, then slowly separate them. While lowering them make two half-circles with your legs, bringing them together 4 inches off the floor. Hold 3 seconds and return to the first position, with knees over chest. Repeat exercise 4 times. After several weeks, add 4 more.

42

43

44

8. KNEE BENDS—FEET APART

Having strong legs is important to keep you from tiring easily. Doing knee bends with feet apart not only strengthens your legs, it stretches the inner-thigh muscles. Also, as your stomach gets larger, keeping your legs apart helps to balance you.

Now stand with feet apart, arms straight out in front of you. Bend your knees, and lower your body as far as you can, then return to a standing position. Try to keep your heels on the floor. Repeat 8 times. Work up to 16 times.

9. KNEE BENDS—SIDE TO SIDE

Stand with feet apart, hands at sides. Bend right knee and lean weight on right leg while keeping left leg straight. Now stand straight and then bend left knee and lean weight on left leg while keeping right leg straight. Repeat 16 times.

10. ARM SWING

Stand with feet apart, arms outstretched at shoulder height. Keeping the hips still, swing your arms from side to side. Let your head follow your arms. Do 16.

48

49

11. WASHING MACHINE

Keeping your feet apart, bend your arms in at the elbows and lean forward at the hip. Twist upward from waist, moving side to side as if you were a washing machine agitating. Do 16.

12. DONKEY KICK—KNEE TO NOSE

Get on your hands and knees, keeping arms straight. Bring right knee under body, up to touch nose, while lowering head; now kick leg out behind you and lift your head. Repeat 4 times and change legs. Do series twice.

50

51

52

53

13. PAINT THE WALL

As in no. 12, get on your hands and knees. As if you had a bucket of paint on your left side, and a paintbrush and a wall to paint on your right, reach your right hand under your left side, then swing your arm out and up to the right side. Repeat 4 times and change sides. Repeat series twice.

14. PRONE ARM LIFTS

Do this exercise until your growing stomach makes you uncomfortable.

Lie prone with your chin on the floor, and your arms outstretched in front of you. Now lift your right arm into the air as far as you can, keeping it next to your ear. Chin remains on the floor. Lower your right arm, then lift the left arm in the same manner. Repeat 16 times.

54

15. PRONE LEG LIFTS

Do this exercise until your growing stomach makes you uncomfortable.

Lie prone, resting your head on folded arms. Keeping your hipbones on the floor, raise the right leg. (Do not bend the knee or let the hipbone off the floor.) Hold leg in the air 2 seconds and then lower it. Raise left leg in the same manner. Repeat 16 times.

16. PRONE—TIGHTEN AND RELEASE

This can and should be continued throughout pregnancy. When your stomach gets large enough to make you feel uncomfortable you may still lie on it by first placing a pillow under your chest and another under your hips. This will take the weight off your stomach.

Lie in a prone position, resting your head on folded arms. Tighten your stomach, buttocks, inner thigh, and vaginal muscles. Hold 4 seconds and release. Repeat 6 times.

Post-Pregnancy

If your doctor permits, you may start exercising the day after your baby is born. You may not feel up to it, but the sooner you start, the better the condition your body will be in. Start your post-pregnancy exercising with a 10-minute program twice a day. As you gain in strength, lengthen your program to 15 minutes twice a day. After 6 weeks you should be able to continue the regular women's program for a half hour to 45 minutes every day.

Start Slowly–While Still in Bed

1. TIGHTEN—RELEASE

Lie supine. (Feel how flat your stomach is? Nice, isn't it?) Pull in your stomach and tighten your buttocks. Hold 4 seconds and release. Repeat 4 times. This exercise should be done often throughout the day, whenever you think of it.

2. RAISE UPPER BODY

Lie supine with arms slightly raised at a 45-degree angle. Start to do a sit-up—stop halfway and return to supine position. Repeat 4 times.

3. KNEE BENDS TO CHEST

a. Lie supine. Bend right knee, lifting foot off bed, then straighten leg and lower to rest on bed. Repeat with left leg. Do each 4 times.

b. As 3a becomes easy, and you are feeling stronger, bring your

56

right knee to your chest, then straighten and lower your leg. Change legs. Repeat with each leg 8 times.

4. SIT-UPS

a. Lie supine, with your arms on the floor above your head. Now swing your arms over your head and bring your body to a sitting position. Slowly lower yourself to original supine position. Repeat 4 times several times a day.

57

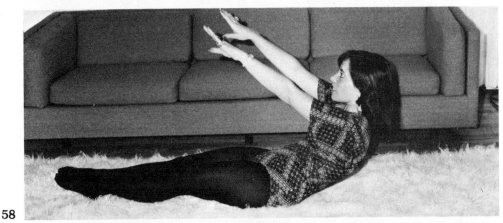

58

59

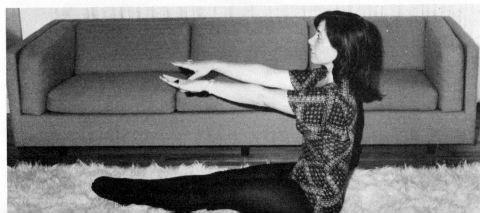

b. After the first week and a half, change the sit-ups slightly. Place your hands behind your neck and pull body into a sitting position. Slowly lower your body to a supine position. Repeat 6 times. This exercise is best done on the floor with your feet tucked under a low chair or couch.

To keep in good shape, you should start doing all the exercises you did before you gave birth. However, if you have stitches, be careful not to do the inner-leg stretches until your stitches are fully healed. Five weeks should be enough time; if not, give yourself another week or two. The better the shape your body's in, the easier it will be to cope with *two* demanding people: your new baby and your adoring husband.

Don't forget to find some time to rest each day.

3

THE CHILDREN'S HOUR

IN THE BEGINNING

During the crucial first years, what a child learns is as important as the food eaten or not eaten. Just as you realize the fetus, an infant, and a growing child require the proper nourishment in order to develop a healthy body and good brain cells, you know they need exercise too. Those years are the child's foundation. Just as one would not build the Empire State Building from the roof down, so one does not develop a healthy body in old age.

Babies should have straight, strong backs and legs. By the time they graduate from cribs, they should have their diplomas of physical fitness. If they do not, they are at a disadvantage, one which will require inordinate efforts to overcome.

With your pediatrician's help, start your infant on the road to a healthy life. Even a tiny baby can be given a gentle exercise program, as you will see from the exercises given later in this chapter.

After the first year of life, a child is on the threshold of taking several giant steps. A foundation has been constructed; now it is time for the first floor. But is the foundation uniformly strong? Are you aware of weak areas? If an area requires reinforcement, can you provide it?

The most important influence on a child's life, up to the early teen years, is the parents. So if you provide positive influences, then your child has definite advantages.

One increasingly competing influence: television! Some programs are good; some bad. I won't mention the bad because enough has been said. Television is often entertaining and educational. From "Sesame Street" a child can learn skills faster than from most other programs. "The Electric Company" is terrific. But all of those wonderful programs do not provide enough physical activity.

WHAT'S AT THE END OF "SESAME STREET"? DOES "THE ELECTRIC COMPANY" SOLVE THE ENERGY CRISIS?

Those programs fill up a time slot here and there, but what about all the other hours? A time for physical activities, usually insufficient in most schools, should be set aside.

The afternoon is a perfect time for mother and child to exercise together. Now, before you grind your teeth, remember: I do not prescribe boring calisthenics! Besides, a child does not have the patience for a military drill.

To begin, set aside special times, twice a week. Try to be consistent, reserving the same time every week. Thirty minutes, each time, is sufficient.

Those times will not only help *you* to stay in shape, but will put your child in shape, too.

Music will make the exercises fun, giving a reason to add some dance. The time will speed along.

You might decide to invite a friend for yourself and one for your child. In other words, do what best suits you and your child.

From such sessions, children not only gain in health, they share in maternal intimacy. In a shared activity, with a common goal, you and your child strengthen a natural bond. In addition, you will soon find your own figure more trim and lovely.

IMMINENT VICTORS

Parents want success, happiness, and health for their children. Bills from doctors, dentists, orthodontists, summer camps, and music teachers may be entered as evidence.

Yet many of the tools your child needs for a good life you can provide yourself with a little time and affectionate interest.

You would not send your child off to school without a nourishing breakfast. Nor should your youngster go through a day without exercise. Physical fitness diminishes the chance of sickness and fatigue; it augments mental alertness and self-confidence. A strong, healthy child is its own best investment.

If that fitness is achieved with Mommy and Daddy, then security and love become additional ingredients.

Such a child will be one of life's long-distance runners, crossing one finish line after another, each a new chapter in success.

So much for mother–child afternoons. How about family weekends?

THE LITTLE LEAGUE IS NOT ENOUGH

Organized sports are wonderful for children. Team spirit and social grace are only two of the benefits. Children generally have a good time venting their aggression and their competitive instincts.

Baseball is great fun for most youths. Yet, baseball does not guarantee physical fitness. Standing in sunny center field waiting for someone to hit a ball is often no more than an exercise in patience.

There must be more; there is more. And daddies can exercise away business lunches, business worries, and exhausting business days. When Mommy joins in, she helps form the most solid of teams: the family team.

Volleyball, soccer, tennis, swimming, skating, skiing, touch football, and jogging are only some of the healthful activities available for the entire family as a unit.

In the following chapters, I shall list activities for family health and categorize them into seasonal activities.

Meanwhile, here are exercises for babies, toddlers, mothers and children, fathers and children, and the entire family.

Babies

Start the exercising as soon as you feel comfortable handling your baby. Some mothers start at one week, others wait a few more. The sooner you start, the better. Building a firm body starts at infancy. A baby kicks and swings its arms wildly, but that does not necessarily provide the proper muscle coordination or tension release that constructive exercising does. Babies love to be handled by their mothers and fathers; it gives them a sense of love and self-confidence.

1. KNEE BENDS

Lay your baby on his back. Take hold of his calves, push his knees to his chest and then straighten his legs. Get a rhythm going back and forth and watch him smile. (Using music makes it more fun.) Repeat 8 times.

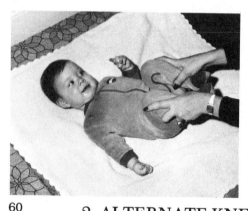 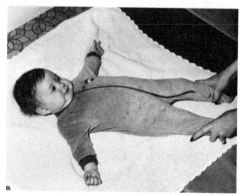

61

60

2. ALTERNATE KNEE BENDS

Keeping your baby on his back, bend the left knee as you straighten the right leg. Alternate by then bending the right knee and straightening the left leg. Again, get a rhythm going. Repeat 8 times.

62

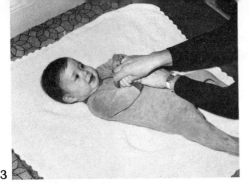

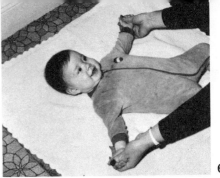

3. ARM CROSS

With your baby on his back, take his hands and cross his arms over his chest, then straighten his arms out to the sides at shoulder level. Repeat 8 times.

4. ARM RAISE

Keeping your baby on his back, take his hands and lower his arms to his sides, then raise his arms over his head. Repeat 8 times.

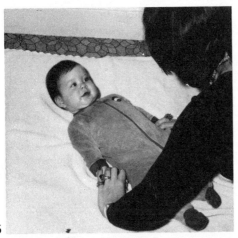

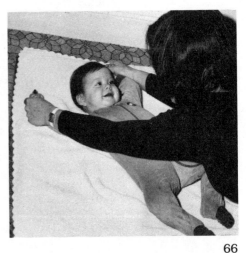

5. ALTERNATE ARM RAISE

As in no. 4, keep your baby on his back and take his hands in yours. Lower one arm to his side while you raise the other over his head. Alternate arms, repeating 12 times.

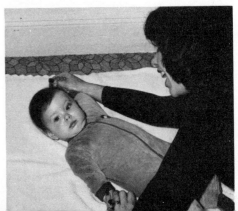

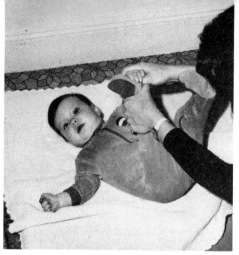

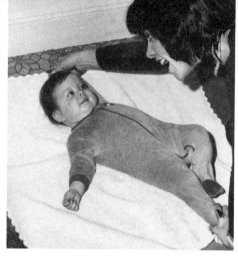

69

68

6. FOOT TO HAND STRETCH

With your baby on his back, take hold of his right calf and left hand. Bring the right foot and left hand together over his stomach and then gently stretch them out. Repeat 4 times and change sides. Repeat 4 times with the left foot and right hand.

7. SIT-UPS

Take your baby's two hands in each of yours and slowly pull him into a sitting position. If your baby cannot hold his head up, place one hand under it to give it support while holding his two hands in your other hand. Once in a sitting position, lower the baby until he is resting on his back. Again, until your baby is strong enough to hold his head up, be sure you give his head support with one of your hands. Repeat 4 times.

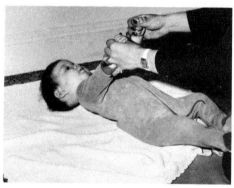

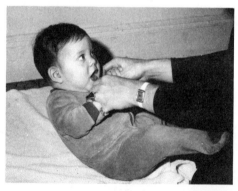

71

70

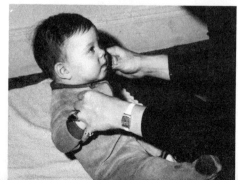

72

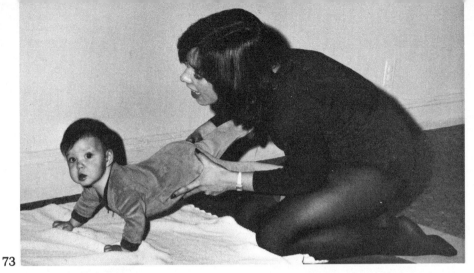

8. PUSH-UP

Now turn your baby on his tummy. Place his hands next to his shoulders and take hold of his hips. Slowly lift his hips a few inches off the floor. At first he will just lie there, but as he gets stronger, he will push up with his arms, placing most of his weight on his hands. He will not be strong enough, in the lower back, to hold his weight, so be sure you are supporting him at his hips, not his legs. Repeat 4 times.

For more baby exercises, get my book *Creative Fitness for Baby and Child*. The above exercises are just a beginning.

TODDLERS

Do these exercises with your child to show him how they are done. It's pleasant and stimulating to exercise outside, but the exercises may be done inside if the weather is poor.

1. SITTING FOOT BOUNCE

Sit with your toddler on the floor or grass. Both of you bend your knees, with feet on floor. Place hands behind you for balance. Now bounce your legs and feet up and down, *off and on* the floor. Repeat 8 to 16 times.

2. SITTING RUN

Keep same position as in no. 1. Bounce one foot at a time, as if you were running in place. Repeat 16 times.

3. ARM SWING

Sit on the floor or grass cross-legged and swing your arms from side to side. Get a rhythm going and repeat 16 times.

75

4. LITTLE–BIG

76

Sit on floor or ground. Curl yourself up as small as possible and then stretch arms and legs out as far as possible. Repeat 8 times. (They love it.)

77

78

5. MONKEY WALK

Get on hands and feet (very young children will automatically get on their knees—try to get them on their feet). Walk around the room or yard in this position. Try keeping your legs as straight as possible. Lean weight equally on hands and feet.

6. JUMP

Jump around the room or yard in one place. Try to get your child to lift both feet at the same time. If he cannot jump with both feet off the ground at the same time, take his hands and help him. After a while he will learn to balance himself correctly in order to do this.

79

7. SCISSORS

Lie on your back with feet up in the air. Keeping legs as straight as possible, spread legs and then bring them together. Repeat 12 times.

8. SIT-UPS

Lie on your back with arms straight back above your head. Swing arms up and over your body, pulling your body into a sitting position. This will be very difficult for the young child, but as he continues trying, he will become strong enough to do it without using his elbow as a crutch. From the sitting position, lower your body SLOWLY to the supine position. Repeat 4 times.

Basic Exercises for Older Children

The children will enjoy doing these exercises outside. If the weather is inclement or outside space is unavailable, exercises should be done indoors.

1. SWIM

Stand with feet apart, bending forward at the hip. Swing your arms as if you were doing the crawl. Use a complete circular motion, alternating first right and then left arm. Repeat 16 times.

2. DEEP KNEE BENDS

Stand with feet together, hands outstretched in front of you. Bend your knees as far as you can to a squatting position and then stand straight. Try to keep your heels on the floor or ground. Repeat 12 times. You might want to take a look at photos 183, 184, and 185.

3. KNEE BENDS—SIDE TO SIDE

Stand with feet apart, hands at sides. Bend right knee and lean weight on right leg while keeping left leg straight. Now stand straight and then bend left knee and lean weight on left leg while keeping right leg straight. Repeat 16 times.

4. FOOT LIFT

Stand with feet together; hands at sides. Raise the right heel; rest on the ball of the right foot. While the right heel is lifted, lean your weight onto the left leg. Now alternate, lifting left heel and leaning on the right leg. Repeat alternation 16 times.

83

5. TOE RAISE

Stand with feet together and hands at sides. Slowly (to the count of 4) rise onto toes (balls of feet). Hold 2 seconds and then lower slowly to flat-footed position. Repeat 6 times.

6. ARM SWING

Stand with feet apart, arms outstretched at shoulder height. Keeping the hips still, swing your arms from side to side. Let your head follow your arms. Do 16.

7. ARM CIRCLE

Stand with feet apart; hands at sides. Now swing arms in a circular motion forward, up, back, and down. Repeat 8 times and change direction, going back, up, forward, and down. Repeat 8 times. Do series three times.

8. SIT-UPS

Sit on the floor or ground with legs straight, placing feet under something sturdy whenever possible. Place hands behind neck. Slowly lie down to a supine position; then, keeping hands behind neck, sit up. Start with 5 and work your way up to 20, adding a few more each week.

9. DONKEY KICK—KNEE TO NOSE

Get on your hands and knees, keeping arms straight. Bring left knee under body, up to touch nose, while lowering head; now kick leg out behind you and lift your head. Repeat 4 times and change legs. Do series twice. For a closer look, see photos 50 and 51.

93

94

10. PAINT THE WALL

As in no. 9, get on your hands and knees. As if you had a bucket of paint on your left side, and a paintbrush and a wall to paint on your right, reach your right hand under your left side, then swing your arm out and up to the right side. Repeat 4 times and change sides. Repeat series twice. Refer to photos 52 and 53 for more detail.

11. RUNNING RACE STARTING POSITION— ALTERNATE LEG JUMP

Lean forward on your hands, with one leg bent under you, and the other stretched out behind you. Keeping both hands on the floor or ground, lean your weight forward and lift both feet off the floor, alternating the position of your legs. Jump in this position, alternating legs, 12 times.

95

96

12. SIDE TO SIDE BOUNCE, SITTING: CHIN TO TOE/EAR TO KNEE

This exercise will not only stretch the back and insides of your legs, it will help stretch backs and upper hip areas.

a. Sit with legs wide apart and straight. Hold right knee, flex foot to give the backs of your leg muscles and tendons greater stretching, and keep head up. Now push torso forward and back. Try to feel as if you were stretching your chin toward your toes. After 8 bounces, change legs. Remember: Keep your chin up.

b. Sit as in *a*, only this time try to pull your ear to your knee without bending the knee. Bounce 8 times and change legs.

Do series *a* and *b* 3 times.

13. LEGS APART HIP LIFT

Sit on the floor or ground with your legs apart and your hands resting flat on the floor behind you. Now push, lifting hips off the floor as high as you can and hold 4 seconds. Then lower to sitting position. Repeat 6 times.

97

14. LEGS APART HIP LIFT—ONE-HANDED

Sit on the floor or ground as in no. 13. This time, rest one hand behind you and keep the other on your lap or knee. As you lift your hips off the floor, reach your free hand into the air, hold 4 seconds and return to a sitting position. Change hands and repeat exercise. Repeat series 4 times.

98

15. KNEE BENDS, HEAD DOWN, STRAIGHTEN

Stand with feet together; hands in front. Bend your knees until you can put your hands on the ground or floor. Keeping your hands on the floor or ground, straighten your legs so that your buttocks are in the air. Hold 4 seconds and return to original standing position. Repeat 8 times.

TOGETHERNESS—PARENT AND CHILD WORKING WITH EACH OTHER

1. ROW YOUR BOAT

Sit on the floor or grass with your child facing you. Spread your legs and have your child do the same. Place your child's feet on the inner side of your knees. Hold hands and rock back and forth, keeping your legs straight. Pull him as far forward as he can go without bending his knees (but not too far, so that you don't cause pain in the back of his legs). Have your child pull you as far forward as you can go, without pain in the back of your legs. You should feel a pulling of the muscles, but not pain. Sing the song "Row, Row, Row Your Boat"; it makes it more fun. Pull back and forth 32 times or for two verses of the song.

100

101

2. BENT KNEE: ROW YOUR BOAT

Sit on the ground or floor with your child facing you. Bend your left leg with its foot resting next to your buttocks. Place your child's right foot on your left knee. Have your child bend his left leg, placing his foot next to his buttocks, and you place your right foot on his left knee. As in no. 1, pull back and forth (sing if you like). Do 16, then change legs. Repeat series two times.

3. PUSH AND PULL

Shoulder to shoulder, stand next to your child, facing in opposite directions. Clasp wrists; place your leg against your child's. As if you were trying to open a heavy door, each of you should push your weight against the other (remember you are bigger, so don't push too hard—push only as hard as the child can bear without falling over). After pushing 4 seconds, still grasping wrists, pull away from each other.

Hold the pull position 4 seconds and return to push position. Repeat
series 6 times and change sides. Repeat 6 times on changed side.

4. HOLDING KNEE BENDS

Take a ¾-inch-thick dowel, 3 feet in length, or a broomstick if you
have no dowel. Face your child. Each of you grasps the dowel (have
your child place his hands between yours). Stand 2 feet away from
each other and slowly do a deep knee bend. Keep heels on the ground
or floor and use each other's weight for balance. Remember: Your
child is not as heavy as you are so don't pull too hard. From the deep
knee bend position, return to standing position. Repeat 8 times.

5. HOLDING DOWEL JUMP

As in no. 4, grasp a dowel or broomstick and face each other. Bend
your knees and tell your child to jump; as the child lands, you jump,
and vice versa. Keep this going 16 times, or longer if you like. It takes
coordination and good timing and is a great deal of fun.

6. SIDE TO SIDE SKIP WITH DOWEL

Face each other, grasping the dowel. As you step to the side with your right foot, your child should step to the side with his left. Then bring your left foot in and your child's right foot. Get a rhythm going (half-jumping with each step) and go across the room or yard in this manner. Do not turn around but recross the yard; this time use the other foot to lead. Watch out for galloping (feet that cross over each other); it is incorrect. Be sure the feet meet and then separate. Start slowly; walk it for a while before you add the skipping motion.

7. JUMP ROPE

a. Each of you take a jump rope (small for your child, longer for yourself). Holding the rope in each hand, let the middle fall onto the floor or ground; now jump over it. Swing your arms back & around and bring the rope in front of you again. Have your child do the same. Until your child can easily jump over the rope, without tangling his feet in it, don't try to jump too quickly. Let the rope fall in front, stop, and then jump. As soon as your child can do this easily, try to get a regular jumping motion going. Try for 10 jumps, without getting tangled in the rope. Then try for 15, then 20.

b. Take your rope and have your child face you, standing very close. Let the rope fall behind your child's feet; both of you should jump as you pull the rope back, up, and around. Again, start this slowly, until you can get a regular jumping pattern going. As the rope hits the ground, tell your child, "JUMP," and you jump as well. It takes awhile, but soon (with patience), you'll be jumping together.

8. WALK UP PARENT'S LEGS:
FLIP OVER BACKWARD

Fun, fun, fun and terrific for self-confidence, flexibility, and strength.

Take hold of your child's hands. Have him lean back and place his shoeless feet upon your legs. Up and up walk little feet on your legs, up to your hips. Then, while you're still holding his hands, let the weight of his legs carry him over backward into a somersault. Do this three or four times and then stop. *Do not* let go during the somersault. Your child will probably want to continue forever, but forever will not be good for your back.

109
110
111

4

SUMMERTIME AND THE LIVIN' IS EEEZEEE

Recalling the summer when I was no more than five years old, I see a little girl in cotton shorts. She was curious, cute, and sometimes clumsy. Her knees and elbows were often decorated with Band-Aids. Her mother was teaching her to ride a small horse; her father had taught her to ski and was beginning to treat her to the excitement of rock-climbing. She took a special joy in swimming, and like a tadpole loved wiggling her little body beneath the surface. Waterskiing was a few years ahead of her.

In addition, that little girl loved to go camping with her parents, eat dinner by the lamp of the moon, then crawl into a sleeping bag under a blanket of stars.

Now, whenever we can, my own family goes camping. It is not only a way of escaping cramped urban life, it lets us swim, canoe, and hike. In fact, it leads back to a time when life was simple and more healthful.

One summer, I found myself trapped in the city, attending a university. After several hours in unairconditioned classrooms, I plunged into New York's cheapest steam bath: the subway. Finally, at home, I drip-dried, having plopped down onto an easy chair, with a cold drink in an airconditioned room. I certainly found going soft, if not plump, an easy task. Within several weeks, I gazed at myself in a mirror, and I nearly moaned out loud. Immediately, I gave up on the subway and used a bicycle. I attended a dance class and went to a nearby pool twice a week. In what seemed like less than no time, I was back in shape. And more than happy to be there.

The urban summer does not force one to choose between the adventures of camping and the lethargy found in an easy chair. Rather, one can combine the best of both worlds.

THE CALL OF THE WILD: CAMPING

I shall never forget my first camping experience. Preparation was argumentative, occasionally chaotic. Setting up our tent, my father tore a gash in the side; while I swung from a nearby branch, my mother was laughing so hard she could barely sew the tear.

However, we soon learned that camping was neither a Mack Sennett comedy nor a Swiss Family Robinson ordeal. During that first day, following a hastily prepared dinner, we retired to our tent. Rain fell with night, and we snuggled into our sleeping bags like caterpillars into cocoons. Day broke with a chorus of birds, and the sun shot shafts of light through leafy trees. It was then that my adventure began.

Before my parents awoke, I scurried out of the tent and monkeyed up an oak. There, I dangled by my knees, scratched and made monkey noises; then I imagined myself hiding from pirates and tigers.

These days, my son behaves much the same way. With self-assurance and brave yells, he moves from branch to branch. And each time he climbs, so does his skill and self-confidence.

Camping, obviously, has been a passion with me. It offers varied opportunities for exploring nature. It is also an opportunity to indulge in a whole variety of outdoor activities. Best of all, it is an activity for the entire family.

ON THE BEACH

If you have neither the time nor the inclination for camping, you may prefer a day on the beach. And if you do, then do not go merely to be roasted by the sun: too much sun is harmful to human skin. Use the time to swim and do simple exercises—many of those the family does at home would be fine. And don't forget a good coating of suntan preparation, one best suited to your skin.

Getting into the Swim

The entire family, from baby up, should be swimming. Of course the ocean is no place to teach a baby, but any pool will suffice. I have been teaching infants, as young as three months, to swim. In fact, babies are particularly good at underwater swimming. And they will prefer that nearly prenatal territory until the age of two years.

But the introduction of a baby to swimming must be gentle; the lessons must be continuously reassuring. Any fear, any doubts will be immediately communicated to the baby. In horror, I once witnessed a woman toss a nine-month-old child into ten feet of water. He sank like a rock. Fortunately, his father saved him; but the poor child was terrified of pools for years.

Swimming is one of the finest, most salubrious exercises in the world. It develops arm and shoulder muscles, back and chest muscles, and leg muscles. If you and your family have not swum during the winter months, I recommend the special warm-up exercises found later in this chapter. Remember: A warmed-up muscle is not only 20 percent more efficient than a cold muscle, it has less chance of being injured.

Different Strokes for Different Folks

Some people swim the backstroke with grace and ease; others swim the butterfly with as little effort as walking. Each of those is a superb muscle developer. Different strokes exercise muscles with varying degrees of pressure. Having done the crawl, one feels quite different from one having done the backstroke. If, after doing the crawl, you suddenly flip over and do the backstroke, you may experience a few minor aches. To get the most from swimming, do several laps of different strokes. Such a program will develop a firm, strong and flexible body.

Of course, swimming laps may become tedious. If you can, have somebody swim along with you. However, if you must swim alone, then try to pace yourself with some lively music.

Make a Splash

In motion, the human body seems capable of transcending itself as it achieves grace under pressure. Yet one cannot dive properly, cannot be graceful, without well-developed muscles. Particularly important is a strong back, capable of arcing ever so slightly. With arms piercing, then floating on air, with legs pushing off like a frog's, then trailing like a rocket's spume, divers achieve awesome movements. Combined swimming and diving will develop endurance, strength, flexibility, and beauty.

So often, children merely fling themselves into water, frequently landing with a clap and a sting. So train them on land first, with warm-up exercises and tumbling, then move to a pool's border. In a short time, they will be fine divers.

The Games People Play

There is Muscle Beach and Bikini Beach. Have you heard of Hot Dog Beach? Or Soccer Sands? Dune Buggy Dunes?

I have often wondered why more beaches are not named for a sport. Though sand sports change from shore to shore, each beach not only accommodates individual activities, but leagues of activities, too. And why not? Beaches are healthful arenas on which everyone may play. They are wonderful spots for families to have fun at volleyball, football, and baseball. If a parent is better than a son or daughter, it makes less difference on a beach than on a more formal playing field.

It is more difficult to jog in sand along the water's edge than on a hard road. It is far more difficult to play volleyball on sand than it is on a carpet of grass. On a road, feet know how they will land, but sand is a shifting material. Therefore, leg muscles are continuously tensing, adjusting to their changing positions. No wonder calf muscles ache after an hour of jogging on the beach!

Following are suggestions for games and activities particularly suitable for beaches. Why not invent some of your own as well?

Make Waves While the Sun Shines: Water Sports

Water, water everywhere. And each drop adds to the splash of fun. One may surf, water-ski, sail, and row. How about volleyball or basketball? All played in water! A variety of land games can be easily transposed to water.

Once in the water, one will have to work harder than on land. For instance, basketball requires a great deal of running and jumping. When running on land you exercise your leg muscles. Basketball in the water utilizes *all* your muscles.

If It "Hertz" to Rent-a-Car, Then Hike, Bike, or Jog

The automobile has, indeed, been a luxury and a convenience. If you are either too lazy or too impatient to walk, then you may slip in behind the wheel, depress the accelerator, and drive off. I do not disparage the automobile: in cars, the police arrive faster than they did on horseback; modern fire engines could not be pulled by a team of Clydesdales; and ambulances have been of incalculable assistance in saving lives. All in all, the internal-combustion engine has been of inestimable value. Yet, like everything else, it has its place. And doctors have yet to invent an engine to replace the heart.

If you are not a regular exerciser, the easiest way to begin is to walk. At first, just a short walk. Maybe twenty minutes. Then, after several weeks, increase your time. Perhaps you will feel comfortable with an hour of walking, perhaps two. Yet, never let yourself become fatigued! After six weeks, try even more exercise; but again, know your limits; check with your doctor.

Having become a walker, try jogging. If you do not want to change suddenly from walking to jogging, you may integrate the two. For instance, walk for twenty minutes, jog for ten. Eventually you should be able to increase your jogging time, developing endurance. As I noted earlier, one's heart is an endurance muscle; therefore, those exercises that are most beneficial to the heart develop and require endurance.

Where to jog? During the summer months, urban sprawl hardly provides the most inviting tracks. Not only is the heat oppressive, but the air is foul. I suggest you either jog at a local Y or out beyond the city limits.

If you have not exercised for some time, have a complete physical examination. Insist on an EKG and know your blood pressure. Your doctor should be able to tell you what and what not to do.

A more adventurous activity is hiking. It is a great family activity and can be part of a camping trip. Put whatever you need into a rucksack; take a walking stick, a compass, and a canteen. Children love to hike, for it means exploring nature. Hiking may include a picnic, fishing, swimming, and a variety of games.

A note of caution: If one hikes in uncharted areas, one should carry an ax for making a path. If you prefer, a thick stick of chalk may be used for marking the barks of trees. A snakebite kit and a first-aid kit are also important precautions. You should not go without them.

CLIMB TO THE TOP OF OLD SMOKEY

Mountains are not only climbed because they exist; they are climbed because we regard them as symbols of things to be conquered. To perch high up on a snowy summit, where the air is cold and dry, is to enjoy one of life's most exciting experiences. To have gotten there, climbing and scaling all the way, is not only invigorating, but full of adventure. Even the preparations for mountain climbing are exciting.

If you decide to try for yourself, you must have strong hands, arms, and legs. A weak back would mean disaster; you should be lithe and well coordinated. Though I do not advise mountain climbing for all, I would suggest many of you give it a try. But remember: Preparedness is the best outfit for such an ascent. And as the poet William Blake sang: "No bird soars too high, if he soars with his own wings."

Neophytes should never venture up by themselves, not even if they possess the necessary physical strength. Instead, they should join an organized group (e.g., The Matterhorn Society, The Alpine Club, etc.). An experienced guide, able to teach, is the best leader for any string of climbers. I won't elaborate on equipment here; there is not much, but it is essential. And an experienced guide will tell you what you need.

Horsing Around

My first horse bit me; my second horse threw me.

Now that I have released your galloping fears, let me rein them in. Riding is not only fun, it is a superb exercise. And a well-trained body easily controls a well-trained horse.

Indeed, horseback riding requires skill only achieved with effort and excellent instruction. Riding requires and develops strong legs and hands; arms must not only be strong, they must be flexible, capable of quick action. As the body moves with the horse, one is exercising. Thigh and calf muscles continuously tighten and relax. So do hands and arms. The back, held straight, develops excellent posture.

One may begin lessons at age five or at age sixty. But remember that an unskilled child, atop an untrained horse, might as well be bouncing on a keg of dynamite. I always advise youngsters starting out to wear a hard hat; precautions never hurt.

Riding is not only an activity for individuals, it can be fun for an entire family. I shall never forget the first time I took my husband and my son riding. My son sat atop an old pony, satisfied with a slow, pensive walk. My husband looked dashing on a great gray mare; however, she wouldn't dash—she merely stood like a statue, while Jeffrey kicked and grimaced. Since then, we have traveled over many trails, and they have all led to a good time.

Tennis Anyone?

Tennis has grown in popularity because it not only provides exercise, it provides an opportunity for keen competition. Once netted, you will have a difficult time abandoning the game; you will always want to improve.

For tennis, you should have a strong grip and strong, agile arms. You must be able to move quickly and easily. These qualities are enhanced by practice. I shall provide you special tennis exercises later in this chapter.

Tennis players perform with greater effectiveness if they warm up just before a game. For much the same reason, you should put on a light sweater or cardigan immediately after a game: quickly cooling muscles are susceptible to chills, causing aches and spasms.

In the Evening

During the summer months, daylight seems to resist the fall of darkness. That expansion of light should be an incentive to adults. If you have worked hard all day, you may look forward to a quiet drink at home before the television set. Yet having sat for ten hours, the body does not need to sit for another four or five; rather, you should be up and about, doing things, enjoying yourself. Now why not consider an evening swim; if a natural body of water is not easily accessible, then how about a pool? People are often surprised at how a tired body snaps to life after a good swim. Or how about tennis? Handball? Jogging? The choices are there; and the choices often make the difference between a long, active life or a short, lethargic one.

An evening out on a dance floor is not only fun, but a form of exercise, too. Dancing for several hours requires endurance, and develops a more enduring heart muscle and good circulation. In fact, all the muscles utilized for dancing are muscles utilized in a variety of exercises.

Remember: An easy chair may be hard on your body.

Summertime Sports

Camping

In order to enjoy the joys of camping, you must be in good shape. Arms, legs, and back must be strong.

Besides doing the exercises listed below, practice using your equipment for several months before you go camping. Fill your pack with all the things you will be taking on your trip and start walking. (If you will only be going on day-pack trips, don't skip over this part. You, too, will get tired, if you're not used to walking long distances with your pack.) Start with 10 minutes around the living room. After the first week, move your walks out-of-doors. Even if you live in a city, get your children to go with you, and be sure they carry packs, too. There is nothing more frustrating than having a child whine, "I'm tired," for three hours of hiking. The child should carry only what is comfortable. At age 6, I had climbed Mt. Washington twice, whining all the way up on the first trip. Knowing better and being stronger the second time, I enjoyed myself. My parents enjoyed me the second time, too! Climbing stairs with your pack on is one of the best exercises to prepare one for mountain climbing or hiking.

You can use your camping equipment for exercise props— lie on your sleeping bag, for example, and use the poles for the tent to steady yourself in place of using a wall.

1. DEEP KNEE BENDS

Stand with feet together, hands outstretched in front of you. Bend your knees as far as you can to a squatting position and then stand straight. Try to keep your heels on the floor. Repeat 12 times. Work up to 25 to 40 deep knee bends.

2. STANDING, SIDE LEG LIFTS

Stand with feet together, resting right hand on the support poles of the tent, or on a tree branch for balance. Holding your body straight and keeping legs straight, raise left leg to the side as high as

112

you can, then lower it. Repeat 8 times and change sides. Do series twice to begin with; after a few weeks make it 4 times.

3. SIT-UPS

With legs straight, sit on the floor or the ground, or your sleeping bag, placing feet under something sturdy whenever possible. Place hands behind neck. Slowly lie down to a supine position; then, keeping hands behind neck, sit up. Start with 5 and work your way up to 20, adding a few more each week.

4. BACK FLAT: LEG LOWER

Lie supine. Bring knees over chest and then straighten legs so they form a 90-degree angle with your torso. Keeping the small of your back pressed against the floor or ground, slowly lower legs. Lower them ONLY as far as you can WITHOUT your back rising off the floor or ground. (If you feel your back rising, you have lowered your legs too far.) When you reach *your* point, hold 4 seconds, then release by bending your knees over your chest. Repeat 4 times. NEVER lower your legs all the way down to the floor or ground as this will cause back strain. Be sure to go only as far as you can, keeping your back FLAT.

5. PRONE ARM LIFT

Lie prone with your chin on your outstretched sleeping bag, and your arms stretched out in front of you. Now lift your right arm into the air as far as you can, keeping it next to your ear. Chin remains on the ground. Lower your right arm, then lift the left arm in the same manner. Repeat 16 times.

6. PRONE LEG LIFT

Lie prone, resting your head on folded arms. Keeping your hip-bones on the ground, raise the right leg. (Do not bend the knee or let the hipbone off the ground.) Hold leg in the air 2 seconds and then lower it. Raise left leg in the same manner. Repeat 16 times.

7. HANDS AND KNEES: FORWARD LEG BOUNCE AND STRETCH

Get on your hands and knees. Place your left foot flat on the ground, *outside* your left hand. Bounce forward and backward, leaning your weight on your left leg. Repeat 8 times and change legs. Do series twice.

113

114

8. KNEE BENDS: HEAD DOWN: STRAIGHTEN

Stand with feet together and arms hanging with hands in front of thighs. Bend your knees, until you can put your hands on the ground. Keeping your hands on the ground, straighten your legs, so that your buttocks are in the air. Hold 4 seconds; return to original, standing position. Repeat 8 times. You may also want to take a look at photo 99.

115

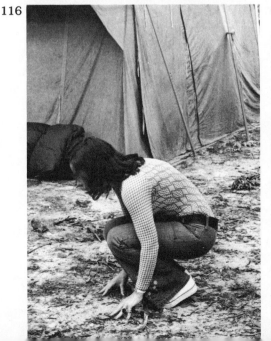

116

117

118

9. STANDING FORWARD BOUNCE

Stand with feet apart, legs straight, and hands clasped behind you. Bounce forward from the hips as far as you can, without bending your knees. Bring your hands up behind you as you bounce. Bounce 8 times forward; 8 times over your right leg; 8 times forward; 8 times over the left leg, and 8 times forward again. Be sure to keep your legs straight. Photo 182 also details this exercise.

10. STANDING: FORWARD STRETCH: ARM TWIST

Stand with feet apart; bend forward from the hips. Keeping your legs straight, place your right hand on your left foot, and your left hand in the air. Now twist your body so that you bring your left hand down to touch your right foot, and stretch your right hand into the air. Twist 16 times, keeping your legs straight.

119

120

Swimming

Besides doing these exercises indoors to warm up for the swimming season, exercising beside the pool or on the beach will be a great inspiration.

1. SWIM

Stand with feet apart; bend forward from the hips. Swing your arms as if you were doing the crawl. Use a complete circular motion, alternating first right and then left arm. Repeat 16 times.

121

122

2. OVERHEAD ARM: BOUNCE SIDE TO SIDE

Stand with feet apart. Raise left arm. Stretch and arc left arm over head and bounce to the right; keep hand flexed as if you wanted to place its palm on a wall on the right. Bounce 16 times and change arms. Repeat same series 8 times, then 4 times, then 2 times.

123

124

125

126

127

3. AIRPLANE STRETCH

Stand with feet apart, fingertips touching in front of chest and elbows sticking out at sides at shoulder height. Bring your elbows back behind you as far as you can, then return to first position. Now straighten your arms (still keeping them at shoulder height); place your palms up, and stretch your arms back as far as you can. Return to starting position. Repeat series 16 times.

4. ARM SWING

Stand with feet apart, arms stretched out at shoulder height. Swing arms from right to left, letting your head follow your arms, but keeping your hips still. Swing 16 times.

5. ARM CIRCLE

Stand with feet apart, arms hanging at sides. Raise arms, swinging in a circular motion, forward, up, backward, and down. Repeat 8 times and change directions, swinging backward, up, forward, and down. Repeat 8 times. Do series twice.

6. BACKSTROKE: HAND TO CHEEK

Stand with feet together, or apart. Raise your left hand; place the back of hand on your left cheek, sticking elbow in the air. With a circular motion, reach behind you and bring your hand down to your thigh. Change hands. Repeat 8 times.

128

129

7. DEEP KNEE BENDS

Stand with feet together, arms outstretched in front of you. Bend your knees as far as you can to a squatting position, and then stand straight. Repeat 12 times.

8. SIDE TO SIDE, DEEP, DEEP KNEE BENDS

a. This looks much easier than it is and is terrific for your legs. Stand with feet apart, arms raised at a 45-degree angle from your sides. Bend your left knee, leaning all your weight on your left leg and lowering your body until you are in a half-squatting position. (Right leg should remain straight.) Now stand straight. Repeat with the right leg. Do 6 times.

b. When 8a becomes manageable (you don't feel as if you will fall over), bend your right leg all the way down as you did before; instead of returning to a standing position stay in the squat position and switch your weight to your left leg, bending the left knee and straightening the right leg. Move slowly or you'll fall over. Move back and forth from right to left, 8 times. Stand straight and shake out your legs to relax the muscles.

130

9. PRONE ARM LIFTS

Lie prone with your chin on the floor or ground and your arms outstretched in front of you. Lift your right arm into the air as far as you can, keeping your arm close to the right side of your head. And keep your chin on the floor or ground. Now lower your arm, then lift the left arm in the same manner. Repeat 16 times.

10. PRONE LEG LIFT

Lie prone, resting your head on folded arms. Keeping your hipbones on the floor or ground, raise the right leg. (Do not bend the knee or let the hipbone leave the floor.) Hold leg in the air, then lower it. Raise left leg in the same manner. Repeat 16 times.

11. ALTERNATE PRONE LEG AND ARM LIFTS

Lie prone, with your chin on the floor or ground and your arms outstretched in front of you. Keeping your arm close to your head, as in no. 9, and your hipbone on the floor, as in no. 10, lift the right arm and the straight left leg; hold 2 seconds and return arm and leg to floor. Change sides, lifting the left arm and the straight right leg. Repeat 8 times.

131

132

133

134

12. LEAN ON ELBOWS: FROG KICK

Sit on the floor or ground; lean back on your elbows and forearms. Bend your knees and bring them up to your chest. Part knees and place soles of feet together. Now part your feet, straightening legs out to the sides. Now scissor your legs back together, keeping feet 24 inches above the floor or ground. Return to bent-knee-over-chest position and repeat 8 times. If this exercise strains your lower back, wait a few weeks until you are stronger and then try it again.

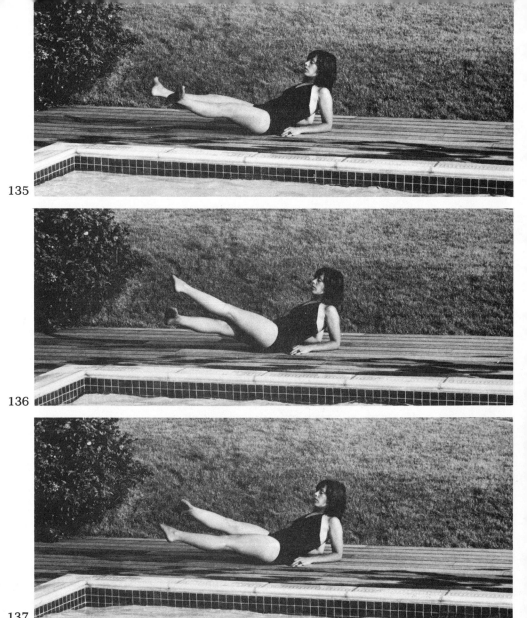

135

136

137

13. LEAN ON ELBOWS: CROSS-OVER SCISSORS

Sit on the floor or ground; lean back on your elbows and forearms. Keeping legs apart, now lift them off the floor with your feet flexed and turned outward. Now turn your feet inward; keeping legs straight, cross your feet in front of you, right leg over left leg. From crossed position, turn feet outward, and return legs to spread position. Be sure *not* to put your feet or legs on the floor or ground. Now turn feet inward again and cross them in front of you; this time left leg over right leg. From crossed position, turn feet outward and return to spread legs position. Repeat 8 times. (If this hurts your lower back or stomach, wait a few weeks before trying this exercise again.)

14. ON ELBOWS, BICYCLE

Sit on the floor or ground; lean back on your elbows and forearms. Bring right knee to chest and lift left leg off the floor, with left foot no more than 5 inches above floor or ground. In a circular motion, as if you were riding a bicycle, alternate the left knee up to your chest while straightening the right leg; now do it vice versa. Do 12 times.

Diving

Do all the swimming exercises to get in shape for water sports, but add the following for flexibility and strength in diving. The photos for this chapter were shot on a diving board for fun *only*. When doing the exercises, they should be done on a firm surface, or you might end up in the water unexpectedly.

1. KNEE BENDS: THEN HEAD DOWN: HANDS ON FLOOR AND STRAIGHTEN LEGS

Stand with feet together and arms hanging with hands in front of thighs. Bend your knees, until you can put your hands on the floor or ground. Keeping your hands on the floor straighten your legs, so that your buttocks are in the air. Hold 4 seconds; return to original, standing position. Repeat 8 times.

2. STANDING FORWARD BOUNCE

Stand with feet apart, legs straight, and hands clasped behind you. Bounce forward from the hips as far as you can, without bending your knees. Keeping your arms straight, bring your hands up behind you as you bounce forward. Bounce 8 times forward; now 8 times over your right leg; now 8 times forward; now 8 times over your left leg; and finally 8 times forward again. Be sure to keep your legs straight. Do series twice.

3. JUMP, LANDING IN A SQUAT POSITION. JUMP, STANDING WITH ARMS OUTSTRETCHED

Stand with feet together and arms at sides. Jump, landing in a squat position; make yourself as small as you can. You may rest your

138

139

hands on the floor or ground. Now jump as hard and as high as you can, landing in a standing position with feet apart and arms outstretched at a 45-degree angle from your shoulders. Repeat 12 times.

4. STRETCH

Stand with feet together, arms stretched upward. Bend the right leg at the knee and stretch your right arm higher above your head, as hard and as far as you can. Hold 4 seconds. Now relax the right arm, still holding it above your head and straighten your right leg. Do the same with your left leg and left arm. Repeat 8 times.

140

Riding

Woe to the unsuspecting person mounting a horse without first preparing one's body. It's not the hour or two of pleasure from galloping around a ring, through fields, or along a beach that should worry one; rather, one might be worried about aching muscles the next day. One might feel a nearly unbearable pain in formerly untroubled areas.

As a teenager, I was an avid rider. And proud of my equestrian ability, I believed my muscles were born to ride. Fifteen years after I had stopped my regular riding, I decided to start again. Being in fine condition, I regarded my body as primed for riding. I rode beautifully for hours and loved it. But the next day my leg muscles were in shock!

These days, I never forget to strengthen muscles needed for a new activity. Following are exercises that should make riding not only an enjoyable event, but an enjoyable memory, too.

1. DEEP KNEE BENDS

Stand with feet together, arms outstretched in front of you. Bend your knees as far as you can to a squatting position, and then stand straight. Repeat 12 times.

2. SITTING ON CHAIR: TIGHTEN RELEASE LEGS

Straddle a chair, facing the back of it. Keep your feet on the floor or ground and your knees bent. Press the sides of the chair with your legs; now tighten all the muscles in your knees and inner thighs. Hold position for 6 seconds, then release. Repeat 6 times. Work up to 12 times.

143

3. PELVIC TILT

Stand with feet apart and knees bent. Place hands on thighs. Without moving legs or upper back and shoulders, stick buttocks out. Now (as if someone came up behind you and slapped your fanny) tuck buttocks under and tighten stomach muscles quickly. Stick buttocks out again, but do *not* move your legs, upper back or shoulders. Repeat 8 to 16 times.

4. ON ELBOWS, KNEES TO CHEST, STRAIGHTEN AND CIRCLE

This is a very difficult exercise and requires strong stomach muscles.

Lean back on elbows and forearms. Bend both knees up to chest. Straighten legs up in the air, then slowly separate them. While lowering them make two half-circles with your legs, bringing them together 4 inches off the floor or ground. Hold 3 seconds and return to the first position, with knees over chest. Repeat exercise 4 times. After several weeks, add 4 more.

5. SIT-UPS

Sit on the floor or grass with legs straight, placing feet under something sturdy whenever possible. Place hands behind neck. Slowly lie down to a supine position; then, keeping hands behind neck, sit up. Start with 5 and work your way up to 20, adding a few more each week.

6. LEAN ON ELBOWS, CROSS-OVER SCISSORS

Sit on the floor or ground; lean back on your elbows and forearms. Keep legs apart, lift them off the floor or grass with your feet flexed and turned outward. Now turn your feet inward; keeping legs straight, cross your feet in front of you, right leg over left leg. From crossed position, turn feet outward, and return legs to spread position. Be sure *not* to put your feet or legs on the floor or ground. Now turn feet inward again and cross them in front of you; this time left leg over right leg. From crossed position, turn feet outward and return to spread legs position. Repeat 8 times. (If this hurts your lower back or stomach, wait a few weeks before trying this exercise again.)

7. ON SIDE—UNDER LEG LIFT

Lie on your left side, resting your head on your left arm, which is stretched above your head. Bend your right leg, placing your right foot behind your left knee. Now, lift your left leg as far as you can, then lower it. Repeat 6 times, turn over, and do the same on your left side. Repeat series 4 times.

8. STRAIGHT LEG FORWARD BOUNCE, SITTING

Sit on the floor or ground, with legs straight out and feet together. Grasp your calves and pull your body forward, bouncing forward and backward. You should feel the backs of your legs stretching. Bounce 16 times.

9. FORWARD BOUNCE, SITTING: KNEES APART

Sit on the floor or ground. Put one sole of your foot against the other sole. Of course your knees will be bent and apart. Grasp ankles and, keeping back straight, rock your torso forward and back 6 times. Now round your back, and pull your head toward your toes and bounce 6 times. Repeat series 4 times.

144

145

10. ELBOW SNAP

Stand with legs apart, arms bent at elbows and held at shoulder height. Twist torso now twice to the right, now twice to the left. Each time you twist come back to original position. Twist as hard as you can, but don't push so hard you hurt your back. Remember: keep hips still. Repeat 16 times.

146

147

Tennis

Tennis is becoming the most popular sport in the country. It is played indoors and outdoors.

One must have quick reflexes and fine coordination for this

sport. Your mind must make split-second decisions, and your body must be strong and flexible to carry them out. Muscles should be warmed up before each game, no matter how often you play. These exercises can be done right on the tennis court before a game, but should also be done at home weeks before you start your tennis season.

148

1. SWIM

Stand with feet apart, bending forward from the hips. Swing your arms as if you were doing the crawl. Use a complete circular motion, alternating first right and then left arm. Repeat 16 times.

2. HIP WAG

Stand with feet apart and arms slightly raised at your sides. Push your hip to the right, leaning most of your weight on the right leg. Now change direction, pushing your hip to the left and leaning most of your weight on the left leg. (Be sure not to stick your buttocks out.) Keep wagging your hips from right to left, keeping the upper half of your body still. Repeat 20 times.

3. SIDE TO SIDE, DEEP, DEEP KNEE BENDS

a. This looks much easier than it is; it is terrific for your legs. Stand with feet apart, arms raised at a 45-degree angle from your sides. Bend your left knee, leaning all your weight on your left leg and lowering your body until you are in a half-squatting position. (Right leg should remain straight.) Now stand straight. Repeat with the right leg. Do 6 times.

b. When *a* becomes manageable (you don't feel as if you will fall over), bend your left leg all the way down as you did before. Instead of returning to a standing position stay in the squat position and switch your weight to your right leg, bending the right knee and straightening the left leg. Move slowly or you'll fall over. Move back and forth from right to left, 8 times. Stand straight and shake out your legs to relax the muscles.

4. ARM SWING

Stand with feet apart, arms stretched out at shoulder height. Swing arms from right to left, letting your head follow your arms, but keeping your hips still. Swing 16 times.

5. OVERHEAD ARM: BOUNCE SIDE TO SIDE

Stand with feet apart. Raise left arm. Stretch and arc left arm over head and bounce to the right; keep left hand flexed as if you wanted to place its palm on a wall to your right. Bounce 16 times and change arms. Repeat same series 8 times, then 4 times, then 2 times.

152

153

154

156

155

157

6. JUMP SERIES

Stand with legs apart and jump up and down 8 times. Now place feet together and jump 8 times. Repeat once. Now jump in a scissors motion, placing right foot in front of left foot, then jump to the position where left foot is in front of right foot. Jump, alternating foot position, 8 times. Now jump once feet apart; now once feet together. Once with left in front of right. Once with right in front of left. Repeat series 4 times. Now jump down, landing in squatting position. Now leap up from squatting position and jump twice with feet together. Repeat series 4 times. Shake your legs and catch your breath.

7. STRETCH

Stand with feet together, arms stretched upward. Bend the right leg at the knee and stretch your right arm higher above your head as hard and as far as you can. Hold 4 seconds. Now relax the right arm, still holding it above your head, and straighten your right leg. Do the same with your left leg and left arm. Repeat 8 times.

8. SIT-UPS

If doing this exercise indoors, sit on the floor with legs straight, placing feet under a chair or a couch. If doing this exercise at the court, sit on the court with legs straight. Place hands behind neck. Slowly lie down to a supine position; then, keeping hands behind neck, sit up. Start with 5 and work your way up to 25, adding a few more each week.

9. FORWARD BOUNCE, SITTING

Sit on the floor or court with legs straight out and feet together. Grasp your calves and pull your body forward, bouncing forward and backward. Feel the backs of your legs stretching. Bounce 16 times.

10. FORWARD BOUNCE, SITTING: KNEES APART

Sit on the floor or court. Put one sole of your foot against the other sole. Of course your knees will be bent and apart. Grasp ankles and, keeping back straight, rock your torso forward and back 6 times. Now round your back, and pull your head toward your toes and bounce 6 times. Repeat series 4 times.

11. ON ELBOW, LEG LIFT

Lie on your left side, keeping torso off the floor or ground, but leaning on left hip and left elbow and forearm. Keep legs straight.

Now lift right leg, like half a scissor, up and down. Don't let your torso sag toward the floor or ground. Keep toes pointed 6 times; 6 times with foot flexed. Change sides and repeat exercise. Repeat series 3 times.

12. ON ELBOW, BICYCLE

Lie on your left side, keeping torso off the floor or ground but leaning on left buttock, left elbow and forearm. For balance, place your right hand on the floor or ground behind you. As if you were riding a bicycle, bend first the left knee, keeping the right leg straight, then bend the right knee, straightening the left leg. Be sure to keep both legs off the floor or ground and keep your body on its side, NOT flat on your buttocks. Repeat bicycle motion 16 times and change sides.

162

13. ON ELBOWS, BICYCLE

Sit on the floor or court, leaning back on your elbows and forearms. Bring right knee to chest and lift left leg off the floor or court, with left foot no more than 5 inches above floor or ground. In a circular motion, as if you were riding a bicycle, alternate the left knee up to your chest while straightening the right leg; now do it vice versa. Do 12 times.

14. LEG BOUNCE

Sit on the floor or court; lean back with arms bent at elbows and rest on your hands. Now bend your knees forming a triangle with your legs and the floor or ground. Now place feet apart. Lift your feet off the floor; now put them on the floor. Now bounce them 25 times. If your stomach muscles begin to hurt, stop and continue later on.

15. WITH RACQUET, ARM SWING

Stand with feet apart. Hold your tennis racquet in front of you horizontally, one hand on the handle, the other on the frame. Keeping your arms at shoulder height, swing them first to the right and then to the left. Keep your arms straight and follow the motion with your head, moving it from side to side. Be sure to keep your hips still. Do 16 times.

16. WITH RACQUET: OVERHEAD, ARM BOUNCE

Stand with feet apart. Hold your racquet horizontally by handle and frame, and raise your arms straight over your head. Keeping your legs straight, lean your torso over your right leg and bounce your torso in an arc-like movement. Keep facing straight ahead so that, as you bounce, you will feel a pull on the left side of your torso. After 4 bounces to the right, change direction and bounce 4 times to the left. Repeat series 4 times.

17. WITH RACQUET, ARM CIRCLE

Stand with feet 6 inches apart. Place your racquet in your right hand. Now swing that arm in a circular motion (keeping it straight) up, back, and down. Repeat 6 times and change circular direction, going back, up, and down. Repeat 6 times and then place your racquet in your left hand. Repeat exercise. Do series 4 times.

Frequently rest and release your muscles during the next set of exercises (19, 20, 21, and 22) by doing the following:

18. WITH RACQUET FORWARD BOUNCE (STANDING)

Stand with feet apart; hold your racquet horizontally in both hands, behind you, by the handle and the frame. Keeping legs straight, bounce forward from the hips and lift your arms up behind you as far as they will go. Bounce forward 8 times; bounce over right leg 8 times; bounce over left leg 8 times; and lastly forward 8 times. Repeat this entire series after each of the following exercises.

19. JUMP, LANDING IN A SQUAT POSITION: JUMP, STANDING WITH ARMS OUTSTRETCHED

Stand with feet together and arms at sides. Jump, landing in a squat position; make yourself as small as you can. You may rest your

171

172

hands on the floor or court. Now jump as hard and as high as you can, landing in a standing position with feet apart and arms outstretched at a 45-degree angle from your shoulders. Repeat 12 times.

20. HOP—JUMP

Hop on your right foot once. Then jump to feet-apart, legs-spread and bent position. Then, hop on your left foot once, then jump to feet-apart, legs-spread and bent position. Repeat 20 times.

173

174

21. RUN IN PLACE

Do exactly as the title says—for three minutes.

22. RUN FORWARD: JUMP-STOP

Run forward 5 steps, then stop suddenly by jumping with feet apart. Start your first run with the right leg, the second run with your left leg. Alternate starting leg each time. Do 16 times.

Team Sports

Almost everyone likes at least one kind of team sport. I've made a list of some, and I'm sure you can add a few too. The exercises that follow are important to the full enjoyment of every sport listed. Keeping muscles strong and flexible will not only lessen the chance of pulling muscles, it will make any sport more enjoyable.

BASEBALL, VOLLEYBALL, BASKETBALL, SOCCER, TOUCH FOOTBALL, MONKEY IN THE MIDDLE, SPUD, KICK THE CAN, CAPTURE THE FLAG, TUG-O'-WAR, KICK BALL, FOX AND HOUNDS, RELAY RACES, ETC.

1. SWIM

Stand with feet apart; bend forward from the hips. Swing your arms as if you were doing the crawl. Use a complete circular motion, alternating first right and then left arm. Repeat 16 times.

2. HIP WAG

Stand with feet apart and arms slightly raised at your sides. Push your hip to the right, leaning most of your weight on the right leg. Now change direction, pushing your hip to the left and leaning most of your weight on the left leg. (Be sure not to stick your buttocks out.) Keep wagging your hips from right to left, keeping the upper half of your body still. Repeat 20 times.

3. KNEE BENDS, SIDE TO SIDE

Stand with feet apart, hands at sides. Bend right knee and lean weight on right leg while keeping left leg straight. Now stand straight and then bend left knee and lean weight on left leg while keeping right leg straight. Repeat 16 times.

4. DEEP KNEE BENDS

Stand with feet together, hands outstretched in front of you. Bend your knees as far as you can to a squatting position and then stand straight. Try to keep your heels on the floor. Repeat 12 times.

5. CURL FEET—FLATTEN

Stand with feet together, hands hanging by thighs. Lean on the outside of your feet and curl your toes under, hold 4 seconds and then relax your toes, letting the feet return to their natural position. Repeat 8 times.

6. SIT-UPS

Sit on the floor or ground with legs straight, placing feet under something sturdy whenever possible. Place hands behind neck. Slowly lie down to a supine position; then, keeping hands behind neck, sit up. Start with 5 and work your way up to 20, adding a few more each week.

7. ON ELBOWS, BICYCLE

Good for stomach and lower-back strength.

Sitting on the floor or grass, lean on elbows and forearms. Pretend you are pedaling a bike. As you bring your right knee up to your chest, lift straight left leg 5 inches off the floor. Now bring your left leg up and straighten the right one (but don't rest it on the floor). Get a smooth circular motion going. Do 16. See Photo 40 in addition to 175.

175

176

177

8. FORWARD BOUNCE, SITTING

Sit on the the floor or ground. Put one sole of your foot against the other sole. Of course your knees will be bent and apart. Grasp ankles and, keeping back straight, rock your torso forward and back 6 times. Now round your back, and pull your head toward your toes and bounce 6 times. Repeat series 4 times. Photos 144 and 145 exhibit this exercise also.

9. SIDE TO SIDE BOUNCE, SITTING: CHIN TO TOE/EAR TO KNEE

This exercise will not only stretch the backs and insides of your legs, it will help stretch backs and upper hip areas.

a. Sit with legs wide apart and straight. Hold right knee, flex foot to give the backs of your leg muscles and tendons greater stretching, and keep head up. Now push torso forward and back. Try to feel as if you were stretching your chin toward your toes. After 8 bounces, change legs. Remember: Keep your chin up.

b. Sit as in *a*, only this time try to pull your ear to your knee without bending the knee. Bounce 8 times and change legs.

Do series *a* and *b* 3 times.

178

179

180

181

10. INFINITY LEG SWING

Sit on the floor or grass; lean back on your elbows and forearms. Stretch your legs out in front of you. Lift right leg, flexing its foot. Now turn foot to the left. Cross your right foot over your left leg. Place the right big toe on the floor or ground on the outer side of your left leg. (If you have to bend your knee a little, do so.) Now twist the right foot, so that the little toe (foot is still flexed) is turned right. Bring your right leg back over the left, bending your knee a bit, placing the right little toe on the floor or grass. Repeat 6 times and change legs.

11. PRONE ARM LIFT

Lie prone with your chin on the floor or ground and your arms outstretched in front of you. Now lift your right arm into the air as far as you can, keeping it next to your ear. Chin remains on the floor or ground. Lower your right arm, then lift the left arm in the same manner. Repeat 16 times.

12. PRONE LEG LIFT

Lie prone, resting your head on folded arms. Keeping your hipbone on the floor or ground, raise the right leg. (Do not bend the knee or raise the hipbone off the floor or ground.) Hold leg in the air 2 seconds and then lower it. Raise left leg in the same manner. Repeat 16 times.

13. DONKEY KICK—KNEE TO NOSE

Get on your hands and knees, keeping arms straight. Bring right knee under body, up to touch nose, while lowering head; now kick leg out behind you and lift your head. Repeat 4 times and change legs. Do series twice.

14. PAINT THE WALL

As in no. 13, get on your hands and knees. As if you had a bucket of paint on your left side, and a paintbrush and a wall to paint on your right, reach your right hand under your left side, then swing your arm out and up to the right side. Repeat 4 times and change sides. Repeat series twice.

15. RUNNING RACE STARTING POSITION: ALTERNATE LEG JUMP

Lean forward on your hands, with one leg bent under you, and the other stretched out behind you. Keeping both hands on the floor or ground, lean your weight forward and lift both feet off the floor, alternating the position of your legs. Jump in this position, alternating legs, 12 times.

16. KNEE BENDS, HEAD DOWN: STRAIGHTEN

Stand with feet together and arms hanging with hands in front of thighs. Bend your knees, until you can put your hands on the floor or ground, straighten your legs, so that your buttocks are in the air. Hold 4 seconds; return to original, standing position. Repeat 8 times.

17. OVERHEAD ARM: BOUNCE SIDE TO SIDE

Stand with feet apart. Raise right arm. Stretch and arc right arm over head and bounce to the left; keep hand flexed as if you wanted to place its palm on a wall to the left. Bounce 16 times and change arms. Repeat same series 8 times, then 4 times, then 2 times.

18. ARM SWING

Stand with feet apart, arms stretched out at shoulder height. Swing arms from right to left, letting your head follow your arms, but keeping your hips still. Swing 16 times.

19. STANDING FORWARD BOUNCE

Stand with feet apart, legs straight, and hands clasped behind you. Bounce forward from the hips as far as you can, without bending your knees. Bring your hands up behind you as you bounce. Bounce 8 times forward; 8 times over your right leg; 8 times forward; 8 times over the left leg, and 8 times forward again. Be sure to keep your legs straight.

182

20. JUMP SERIES

Stand with legs apart and jump up and down 8 times. Now place feet together and jump 8 times. Repeat once. Now jump in a scissors motion, placing right foot in front of left foot, then jump to the position where left foot is in front of right foot. Jump, alternating foot position, 8 times. Now jump once feet apart; now once feet together. Once with right in front of left. Once with left in front of right. Repeat series 4 times. Now jump down, landing in squatting position. Now leap up from squatting position and jump twice with feet together. Repeat series 4 times. Shake your legs and catch your breath.

5

The Greening of Winter:
Winter Sports for Summer Athletes

If you live in a tropical climate, you may play summer sports from one end of a year to another. But even if you face a frosty winter every year, you never have to stop enjoying sports. You can swim, play tennis and handball, even jog—indoors. Even more exciting: participate in a range of activities that actually require snow and ice.

Hitch a Ride on a Chair Lift (But First Warm Up Your Own Motor)

You do not merely enjoy a winter of weekend skiing, you must get in shape for it. If you do not, the slippery slopes may hit you a lot harder than you hit the slopes.

In order to avoid a broken limb and to keep the right end up, I have prepared a simple series of warm-up exercises for skiers. You should begin them two months before the ski season. A few days each week will put one in shape for almost any slope.

My exercises are not only easy, they are fun, especially when accompanied by music or done in a group. The happy result will be a deep sense of confidence and a comfortable familiarity with skis, poles, and—of course—your own body.

Further, I shall offer instructions for such essential maneuvers as Kick Turns, Herringbones, Snowplowing, Heel Jumps, Edging, Falling, and Sidestepping.

If you have never been on skis, I can help you on and point you downhill. First do my pre-ski exercises, then join a ski school. In short order, it will be downhill all the way.

If you are a skier, I hope to make you a safer skier, as well as a better one.

I should just add that cold-weather sports tend to burn up more calories than warm-weather sports. So as the snow falls, so may one's weight.

GAY BLADES CUT SHARP FIGURES

There are several varieties of ice-skating: racing, pleasure skating, figure skating, ice hockey, and the pleasures afforded couples skating arm in arm. Most of us skate solely for the fun of it. Such skating, though invigorating, utilizes only *some* of our muscles. Those in our legs must not only be strong, they must be agile and flexible, too. Certainly, strong ankles are necessary for controlled skating. In order to develop "ramrod" ankles, one should practice walking in skates, off the ice (and off the living room rug!). Once a hobbling stability has been achieved and the ankles do not bend, you are ready to glide onto the ice.

Later on in this chapter, I shall provide very specific exercises for strengthening ankles, not only for skating, but for skiing, too.

POOLING AROUND

As I stated earlier, swimming is the finest general exercise. Yet in the winter, when steamlike breaths burst from mouths, an immediate plunge into a heated pool may cause one's muscles to tense.

Instead, one should arrive at an indoor pool, change, then spend ten minutes doing warm-up exercises. They are quite easy and may be found with other exercises, later in this chapter.

For a really tough workout, you can do what the famous Florence Chadwick did: at a pool, she would tie herself to the base of a lifeguard's chair. Then she would jump in and swim in place, keeping the rope taut. The exertion was enormous; the benefits were even greater. But this is strenuous, and I don't advise it for everybody.

Snowshoes on Holiday

Large webbed shoes. Deep snow.

As a child in the West, as a teenager in New England, I enjoyed deep winter snows that provided an unusual sense of excitement and freedom. With a friend and my parents, I used snowshoes to explore countrysides unavailable to others. I inhaled pure air, watched and glimpsed animals as amazed to see me in their natural habitats as I was to see them.

If you try snowshoeing, you will experience your own revelations of a vanishing wilderness. Furthermore, snowshoeing (like jogging and hiking) is a superb exercise. It not only requires the exertion of leg muscles, it strengthens the heart, for it is an endurance activity. For a few weeks, before such an undertaking, prime yourself with regular long walks. Familiarize yourself (and your family) with snowshoes. And, of course, do the leg exercises later on in this chapter.

Yet, one should not go marching off alone: if an accident occurs, others should be around to provide assistance.

The Cross-Country Swing

The popularity of cross-country skiing has increased for a number of reasons: no chair lifts, no lines, no waiting. It usually offers an easier way to be outdoors and get exercise than regular downhill skiing. In addition, it is safer because you are less likely to take a dangerous fall. For that reason (and others to follow), it is a superb sport for pregnant women. I know from experience: I taught exercise classes through my eighth month. And I cross-countried with extra baggage in my belly. Of course, every woman should check with her doctor first.

Now what exactly does cross-country skiing entail? You must have a pair of long, narrow skis and a pair of flexible boots, specially manufactured for cross-country use. The poles are regulation size. The snow need not be paved like a road, but a hard-packed snow provides a conducive surface.

Now that you know about the equipment, how about the movements? Arms and legs are in repeated motion, and one's back muscles are constantly used. The motion of the skier resembles a swinging, loping gait. As a result, one uses more muscles more consistently and evenly than in any other variety of skiing.

However, because cross-country skiing employs so many muscles, you should be in excellent condition before starting. Once in shape, cross-country skiing will keep you as fit as a cat. In fact, after several outings, you may be able to cover twenty miles in a day. But begin gradually, doing my exercises, and building up endurance.

WINTER SPORTS

Skiing

For ski exercises, ski boots should be worn when possible.

1. SWIM

Stand with feet apart; bend forward from the hips. Swing your arms as if you were doing the crawl. Use a complete circular motion, alternating first right and then left arm. Repeat 16 times.

2. KNEE BENDS—HEELS DOWN

Stand with feet together, hands outstretched in front of you, perpendicular to the floor or ground. Bend your knees as far as you can to a squatting position and then stand straight again. Keep your heels on the floor. If you cannot keep your heels on the floor while in the squatting position, only bend as far as you can keeping them on the floor. After several weeks you should be able to squat with heels on the floor or ground. Repeat 16 times.

184

183

185

3. KNEE BENDS, SIDE TO SIDE

Stand with feet apart, hands at sides. Bend right knee and lean weight on right leg while keeping left leg straight. Now stand straight and then bend left knee and lean weight on left leg while keeping right leg straight. Repeat 16 times.

4. KNEE WAG

Stand with feet and knees together; arms hanging down at sides. Bend legs at knees, now lean on the outer part of your left foot, inner part of your right foot, and push your knees to the left. Now change direction, leaning on the outer part of your right foot, the inner part of your left foot, and pushing your knees to the right. Keep switching direction, back and forth, 16 times. After two weeks, go up and down slightly as you wag. Do that 16 times also.

186

187

5. PELVIC TILT

Stand with feet apart and knees bent. Place hands on thighs. Without moving legs or upper back and shoulders, stick buttocks out. Now (as if someone came up behind you and slapped your fanny) tuck buttocks under and tighten stomach muscles quickly. Stick buttocks out again, but do *not* move your legs, upper back or shoulders. Repeat 8 to 16 times.

188

189

6. SNOWPLOW

Stand with feet wide apart and turned inward: pigeon-footed. Now bend your knees and tuck your pelvis under and forward. Bend your elbows so that your arms look like chicken wings. Now lean torso over right leg, letting all your weight rest on the right leg. Now change direction, leaning all your weight on your left leg. Change from right to left and left to right 16 times.

7. FORWARD BOUNCE, STANDING

Stand with feet apart, legs straight, and hands clasped behind you. Bounce forward from the hips as far as you can, without bending your knees. Bring your hands up behind you as you bounce. Bounce 8 times forward; 8 times over your right leg; 8 times forward; 8 times over the left leg, and 8 times forward again. Be sure to keep your legs straight.

8. ARM SWING

Stand with feet apart, arms stretched out at shoulder height. Swing arms from right to left, letting your head follow your arms, but keeping your hips still. Swing 16 times.

9. PRONE ARM LIFT

Do this exercise lying prone with your chin on the floor or ground and your arms outstretched in front of you. Now lift your right arm into the air as far as you can, keeping it next to your ear. Chin remains on the floor. Lower your right arm, then lift the left arm in the same manner. Repeat 16 times.

10. PRONE LEG LIFT

Do this exercise lying prone, resting your head on folded arms. Keeping your hipbone on the floor or ground, raise the right leg. (Do not bend the knee or let the hipbone off the floor.) Hold leg in the air, then lower it. Raise left leg in the same manner. Repeat 16 times.

11. BACK FLAT—LEG LOWER

Lie supine. Bring knees over chest and then straighten legs so they form a 90-degree angle with your torso. Keeping the small of your back pressed against the floor or ground, slowly lower legs. Lower them ONLY as far as you can WITHOUT your back rising off the floor. (If you feel your back rising, you have lowered your legs too far.) When you reach *your* point, hold 4 seconds, then release by bending your knees over your chest. Repeat 4 times. NEVER lower your legs all the way down to the floor or ground as this will cause back strain. Be sure to go only as far as you can, keeping your back FLAT.

12. SIT-UPS

Keeping legs straight, placing feet under something sturdy whenever possible, sit on the floor. Place hands behind neck. Slowly lie down to a supine position; then, keeping hands behind neck, sit up. Start with 5 and work your way up to 20, adding a few each week.

13. BENT KNEE SIT-UPS

Follow instructions in no. 12; however, knees must be bent and feet resting on the floor rather than legs outstretched in front of you.

190

14. DONKEY RUN

Bend forward in an arc, placing your hands and feet on the floor or ground. Keep your buttocks up. You do not have to keep your legs straight for this exercise. Now run in place, leaning most of your weight on your hands. Run 24 times.

15. DOUBLE DONKEY HOP

Bend forward in an arc; place your hands and feet on the floor or ground. This time try to keep your legs as straight as possible. Keeping your hands on the floor, hop up and down on your feet. Do not hop higher than three inches. Your weight will be pushed onto your hands, so don't try to hop too high or you'll land on your nose. Remember: Keep your legs straight. Hop 16 times.

191

192

16. MONKEY WALK

Get on your hands and feet (very young children will automatically get on their knees—try to get them on their feet). Walk around the room or yard in this position. Try keeping your legs as straight as possible. Lean weight equally on hands and feet.

17. ON ELBOWS, BICYCLE

Good for stomach and lower-back strength.

Sitting on the floor or ground; lean on elbows and forearms. Pretend you are pedaling a bike. As you bring your right knee up to your chest, lift straight left leg 5 inches off the floor. Now bring your left leg up and straighten the right one (but don't rest it on the floor). Get a smooth circular motion going. Do 16.

18. INFINITY LEG SWING

Sit on the floor or ground; lean back on your elbows and forearms. Stretch your legs out in front of you. Lift right leg, flexing its foot. Now turn foot to the left. Cross your right foot over your left leg. Place the right big toe on the floor or ground, on the outer side of your left leg. (If you have to bend your knee a little, do so.) Now twist the right foot, so that the little toe (foot is still flexed) is turned right. Bring your right leg back over the left, placing the right little toe on the floor. Repeat 6 times and change legs.

19. AIRPLANE STRETCH

Stand with feet apart, fingertips touching in front of chest and elbows sticking out at sides, at shoulder height. Bring your elbows back behind you as far as you can, then return to first position. Now straighten your arms (still keeping them at shoulder height); place your palms up, and stretch your arms back as far as you can. Return to starting position. Repeat series 16 times.

20. STRETCH (OVERHEAD)

Stand with feet together, arms stretched upward. Bend the right leg at the knee and stretch your right arm higher above your head as hard and as far as you can. Hold 4 seconds. Now relax the right arm, still holding it above your head and straighten your right leg. Do the same with your left leg and left arm. Repeat 8 times.

21. SNOWPLOW—KNEE BEND

Stand with feet apart and turned inward: pigeon-footed. Keep calves apart, yet knees and thighs together. They should form a triangle with the floor or ground. Now release legs, unbend them till straight. Repeat 16 times.

193

194

PUT YOUR SKIS ON. BE SURE YOU ARE IN A CLEAR AREA, whether indoors or outdoors.

22. TIP, TIP SKI RUN

With your skis on, running in place develops the proper muscles for downhill skiing.

Stand with feet together (i.e. skis parallel) and poles at your sides. Your arms should be bent, elbows pointing back. Now lift the right heel off the ground; as you replace it, lift the left heel off the ground. Now run in place with your skis on. Use poles for balance and be sure to keep the tips of your skis on the ground. Only the heels of the skis should leave the ground. Start with one or two minutes and bring it up to 5.

23. KNEE BEND TO FORWARD STRETCH

Stand with feet together, arms outstretched at 45-degree angles and poles placed on the ground for balance. Do a deep, deep knee bend until your buttocks almost touch the backs of your skis. Remember: Use your poles for balance or you will topple over. Now stand up straight again; place your poles by the tips of your skis and lean forward as far as possible, without bending your knees. Lean your weight on your poles. Repeat 8 times.

199

24. KICK TURN

To turn around in an area not sufficiently large, one must employ the kick turn. This is a good exercise for leg strength, flexibility, balance and coordination.

With skis on, stand with feet together, arms bent. Point elbows backward. Keep hands on tops of vertical poles. To make a right kick turn, place your left pole by the tip of your left ski. Twist your body to the right. Place your right pole by the back of your right ski. Balance your weight on your poles, now lift your right ski off the ground, raising the tip of the ski into the air. The end of the ski will rest on the ground close to the left ski tip. Your right leg should be straight out in front of you; parallel to the ground. Ski should be perpendicular to the ground. Now twist your foot to the right letting your ski swing around until your feet are together pointing in opposite directions: the right boot's toe next to the left heel. Now lift your poles and your left leg, swinging your left ski around to rest parallel to the right ski. Place poles in the start position. To make a left kick turn, do just the opposite. At first, you will probably get tangled in skis and poles; but as you practice, kick turns will become easy.

200

201

202
203

Exercises 25 and 26 can be done indoors months before the ski season, but *must* be done outdoors, minutes before you start skiing.

25. HERRINGBONE

The best way to get up a hill is the herringbone.

Stand with feet apart; the heels of your skis almost touching, the tips of your skis wide apart. Hold your poles at your sides. Now lean the weight of your body on the inside of your feet so that your ankles bend inward and upward. The outside of your skis will come off the ground. Begin to walk forward in this silly position. As you place your right ski forward, place your right arm and pole forward, keeping them on the outer side of the ski. As you place your left ski forward, place your left arm and pole forward. By pressing the ground hard with the inside of your ski, you will not slide backward. When you've reached your destination, bring your skis together, perpendicular to the slope of the mountain. Now press down with the outer edge of the uphill ski and the inner edge of the downhill ski. If you let your skis lie flat against the slope, you will go down the mountain sideways, probably falling as you go.

204

26. SIDESTEP

To climb steep hills, one must know how to sidestep. (Sidestepping is also a great way of warming up your body.)

Stand with skis close together and parallel. To sidestep to the right, lean both your legs to the right, bending the knees and ankles. Now tilt the inner edge of the right ski off the ground, and the outer edge of the left ski off the ground. Your poles should be at your sides. Now lean your weight (enough for balance) on your poles. As you lift your right leg off the ground, lift your right pole off the ground; as you place your right ski on the ground, place your right pole on the ground. Now lift your left ski off the ground; place it next to the right ski on the ground. Now bring the left pole beside you. Do not lift the left pole as you lift your left ski; the left pole will balance you, until both skis are securely in place. Repeat until you reach your destination. If you are doing it for practice on flat ground, repeat 16 times to the right, 16 times to the left.

206

205

207

27. GETTING UP—Practice this one at home. No need to cover yourself with snow before you start your skiing day.

No matter how well you ski, you will fall at one time or another. Some falls are simple, others more complex. In any case, don't PANIC! Try to figure out where your legs are; then check which side of you is downhill, which is uphill. Now try to maneuver yourself onto your back, with your back across the slope, and with BOTH skis in the air. When both skis are in the air, and YOU are lying perpendicular to the slope, let both skis fall to the downhill side of you. Now sit up, raise your arms, and place your poles on the uphill side of your skis. Lift your weight onto your poles; now pull yourself to a standing position. There!

208
209

210

211

212

Skating

1. ARM SWING

Stand with feet apart, arms outstretched at shoulder height. Keeping the hips still, swing your arms from side to side. Let your head follow your arms. Do 16.

2. KNEE BENDS

Stand with feet together, hands outstretched in front of you. Bend your knees as far as you can to a squatting position and then stand straight. Try to keep your heels on the floor or ground. Repeat 12 times.

3. SNOWPLOW—KNEE BEND

Stand with feet apart and turned inward: pigeon-footed. Keep calves apart, yet knees and thighs together. They should form a triangle with the floor or ground. Now release legs, unbend them till straight. Repeat 16 times.

4. KNEE WAG

Stand with feet and knees together; arms hanging down at sides. Bend legs at knees, now lean on the outer part of your right foot, inner part of your left foot, and push your knees to the right. Now change direction, leaning on the outer part of your left foot, the inner part of your right foot, pushing your knees to the left. Keep switching direction, back and forth 16 times. After two weeks, go up and down slightly as you wag. Do that 16 times also.

5. KNEE BENDS: SIDE TO SIDE

Stand with feet apart, hands at sides. Bend right knee and lean weight on right leg while keeping left leg straight. Now stand straight and then bend left knee and lean weight on left leg while keeping right leg straight. Repeat 16 times.

6. FORWARD BOUNCE: STANDING

Stand with feet apart, legs straight, and hands clasped behind you. Bounce forward from the hips as far as you can, without bending your knees. Bring your hands up behind you as you bounce. Bounce 8 times forward; 8 times over your right leg; 8 times forward; 8 times over the left leg, and 8 times forward again. Be sure to keep your legs straight.

7. STANDING GOOSE-KICK

Stand with feet apart, arms outstretched in front of you, at shoulder height. Bend left leg slightly at knee; now, keeping right leg straight, kick it up so that the foot touches left hand. Now kick left leg to right hand, slightly bending right knee. Do 16 times.

8. OVERHEAD: ARM BOUNCE—SIDE TO SIDE

Stand with feet apart. Raise left arm. Stretch and arc left arm over head and bounce to the right; keep hand flexed as if you wanted to place its palm on a wall to the right. Bounce 16 times and change arms. Repeat same series 8 times, then 4 times, then 2 times. See photo 126.

9. FLAMINGO KNEE BEND
(ONE-LEGGED KNEE BEND)

This is a killer, even if you're not an endangered species. Stand on your right foot; now lift your left foot, 10 to 12 inches off the floor or ground, as if it were kicking. Hold the kick pose. Now with all your weight on your right leg, bend your right knee, lowering your body as far as you can. Remember: Keep your left leg OFF the floor or ground out in front. Now raise yourself.

Don't go too far down at first, or you won't be able to stand without using both legs. Do 4 times on each leg. As you get stronger, you'll be able to go lower and lower, until your buttocks almost touch the floor. But don't be in a hurry. Your legs will get stronger week by week. And don't worry if you can't get up the first time.

10. SIT-UPS

Sit on the floor or ground with legs straight, placing feet under something sturdy whenever possible. Place hands behind neck. Slowly lie down to a supine position; then, keeping hands behind neck, sit up. Start with 5 and work your way up to 20, adding a few more each week.

11. FLAT BACK: LEG LOWER

This exercise is essential for lower-back strength.

Lie supine. Bring knees over chest and then straighten legs so they form a 90-degree angle with your torso. Keeping the small of your back pressed against the floor or ground, slowly lower legs. Lower them ONLY as far as you can WITHOUT your back rising off the floor or ground. (If you feel your back rising, you have lowered your legs too far.) When you reach *your* point, hold 4 seconds, then release by bending your knees over your chest. Repeat 4 times. NEVER lower your legs all the way down to the floor or ground as this will cause back strain. Be sure to go only as far as you can, keeping your back FLAT.

Snowshoes

1. KNEE BENDS

Stand with feet together, hands outstretched in front of you. Bend your knees as far as you can to a squatting position and then stand straight. Try to keep your heels on the floor. Repeat 12 times.

2. KNEE BENDS: SIDE TO SIDE

Stand with feet apart, hands at sides. Bend right knee and lean weight on right leg while keeping left leg straight. Now stand straight and then bend left knee and lean weight on left leg while keeping right leg straight. Repeat 16 times.

3. RUN IN PLACE

Do exactly as the title says—for three minutes.

4. JUMP ROPE

Take a jump rope. Holding it in each hand, let the middle fall onto the floor or ground. Now jump over it. Swing your arms up behind you and swing the rope over your head. Now get a regular jumping motion going. Do ten jumps the first week, working your way to 15, and then to 20.

5. AIRPLANE STRETCH

Stand with feet apart, fingertips touching in front of chest, and elbows sticking out at sides, at shoulder height. Bring your elbows back behind you as far as you can, then return to first position. Now straighten your arms (still keeping them at shoulder height); place your palms up, and stretch your arms back as far as you can. Return to starting position. Repeat series 16 times.

6. FORWARD BOUNCE: STANDING

Stand with feet apart, legs straight, and hands clasped behind you. Bounce forward from the hips as far as you can, without bending your knees. Bring your hands up behind you as you bounce. Bounce 8 times forward; 8 times over your right leg; 8 times forward; 8 times over the left leg, and 8 times forward again. Be sure to keep your legs straight.

7. SIT-UPS

Sit on the floor or ground with legs straight, placing feet under something sturdy whenever possible. Place hands behind neck. Slowly lie down to a supine position; then, keeping hands behind neck, sit up. Start with 5 and work your way up to 20, adding a few more each week.

8. ON ELBOWS, BICYCLE

Good for stomach and lower-back strength.

Sitting on the floor or ground, lean on elbows and forearms. Pretend you are pedaling a bike. As you bring your right knee up to your chest, straighten left leg (but don't rest it on the floor). Now bring your left leg up and straighten the right one. Get a smooth circular motion going. Do 16.

9. ON ELBOWS, KNEES TO CHEST: STRAIGHTEN LEGS AND CIRCLE

This is a very difficult exercise and requires strong stomach muscles. If you are new to exercise, wait a few weeks before adding this one to your daily program.

Lean back on elbows as in no. 8. Bend both knees up to chest. Straighten legs up into the air, then slowly separate them. While lowering them, make two half-circles with your legs, bringing them together 4 inches off the floor or ground. Hold 3 seconds and return to the first position, with knees over chest. Repeat exercise 4 times. After several weeks, add 4 more.

10. DONKEY RUN

Bend forward in an arc; place your hands and feet on the floor or ground. Keep your buttocks up. You do not have to keep your legs straight for this exercise. Now run in place, leaning most of your weight on your hands. Run 24 times.

11. RUNNING RACE, STARTING POSITION: ALTERNATE LEG JUMP

Lean forward on your hands, with one leg bent under you, and the other stretched out behind you. Keeping both hands on the floor or ground, lean your weight forward and lift both feet off the floor, alternating the position of your legs. Jump in this position, alternating legs, 12 times.

Cross-Country Skiing

1. DEEP KNEE BENDS

Stand with feet together, hands outstretched in front of you. Bend your knees as far as you can to a squatting position and then stand straight. Try to keep your heels on the floor or ground. Repeat 12 times.

2. KNEE BENDS: SIDE TO SIDE

Stand with feet apart, hands at sides. Bend right knee and lean weight on right leg while keeping left leg straight. Now stand straight and then bend left knee and lean weight on left leg while keeping right leg straight. Repeat 16 times.

3. RUNNING RACE, STARTING POSITION: ALTERNATE LEG JUMP

Lean forward on your hands, with one leg bent under you, and the other stretched out behind you. Keeping both hands on the floor or ground, lean your weight forward and lift both feet off the floor, alternating the position of your legs. Jump in this position, alternating legs, 12 times.

4. SNOWPLOW—KNEE BENDS

Stand with feet apart and turn inward: pigeon-footed. Keep calves apart, yet knees and thighs together. They should form a triangle with the floor or ground. Now release legs, unbend them till straight. Repeat 16 times.

5. ON ELBOWS, BICYCLE

Good for stomach and lower-back strength.

Sitting on the floor or ground, lean on elbows and forearms. Pretend you are pedaling a bike. As you bring your right knee up to your chest, straighten left leg (but don't rest it on the floor). Now bring your left leg up and straighten the right one. Get a smooth circular motion going. Do 16.

6. GETTING OFF THE RACK

Lie supine with legs outstretched and arms stretched above your head, on the floor or ground. Raise your straight right leg into the air; now swing your arms up over your head and bring your body into a sitting position. While doing that, grab your right ankle in both hands. If you cannot reach your ankle without bending your knee, grab your calf. Now let go of your leg and lower your body to its original position: legs outstretched on the floor and arms outstretched above your head. Repeat exercise, raising the left leg. Do series 8 times.

7. DONKEY KICK—KNEE TO NOSE

Get on your hands and knees, keeping your arms straight. Bring right knee under body, up to touch nose, while lowering head; now kick leg out behind you and lift your head. Repeat 4 times and change legs. Do series twice.

8. PAINT THE WALL

As in no. 7, get on your hands and knees. As if you had a bucket of paint on your left side, and a paintbrush and a wall to paint on your right, reach your right hand under your left side, then swing your arm out and up to the right side. Repeat 4 times and change sides. Repeat series twice.

9. STANDING: FORWARD STRETCH: ARM TWIST

Stand with feet apart; bend forward from the hips. Keeping your legs straight, place your right hand on your left foot, and your left hand in the air. Now twist your body so that you bring your left hand down to touch your right foot, and stretch your right hand into the air. Twist 16 times, keeping your legs straight.

10. FORWARD BOUNCE: STANDING

Stand with feet apart, legs straight, and hands clasped behind you. Bounce forward from the hips as far as you can, without bending your knees. Bring your hands up behind you as you bounce. Bounce 8 times forward; 8 times over your right leg; 8 times forward; 8 times over the left leg, and 8 times forward again. Be sure to keep your legs straight.

11. KNEE BENDS: THEN HEAD DOWN: HANDS ON FLOOR AND STRAIGHTEN LEGS

Stand with feet together and arms hanging with hands in front of thighs. Bend your knees, until you can put your hands on the floor or ground. Keeping your hands on the floor, straighten your legs, so that your buttocks are in the air. Hold 4 seconds; return to original, standing position. Repeat 8 times.

6

HARD TIMES: STRESS AND TENSION

In a stressful situation, most people suffer from a variety of side effects. Tension often manifests itself as a throbbing headache, a stomach cramp, or a daggerlike pain in the back. But those are only the most obvious manifestations.

THE WORST OF TIMES: HARD-HEARTED HEART

On television, on radio, in schools, and in this book, I have often spoken of the heart muscle. More and more people suffer from cardiac disease.

The causes are varied, including smoking, alcohol, fats, and inactivity. Yet few people realize that tension, also, may cause heart damage.

During periods of intense stress and tension, the heartbeat and blood pressure usually increase: the heart is working extra hard, supporting the body during a time of crisis. In *Your Heart and How to Live with It*, mentioned earlier, Dr. Lawrence E. Lamb writes: "The circulatory response is thought to be associated with the outpouring of adrenalin-like substances from the adrenal gland. Chemical substances derived from these secretions are sometimes stored in the heart. Long-term recurrent psychic stress could contribute to changes in heart function."

No wonder so many middle-aged executives, working under intense stress, suffer heart failure. The price of success need not cost so much. Rather, success and good health should be partners in a working relationship.

So, how does one deal with stress and tension? Many

doctors believe the damage caused by some forms of tension may be reduced by a regular exercise program.

GET 'EM TIGER!

Man, perhaps, is the only animal who suffers tension lying down. Among four-legged creatures, tension is never banked, never collects interest: a dog growls; a cat runs. The point, of course, is that they actively react; they are not passive.

Man, unfortunately, not only remains still, but often tries to mask his feelings. At such times, tension may become unbearable: hearts gallop and pulses go wild. And what do humans do? They sit and nibble their nails.

CITY PROBLEMS

In addition to the physical inertia of a technological society, many of us live in noisy, dirty, dangerous cities. If you work at a desk, in a pressurized, competitive environment, you are a candidate for tension.

Yet, you can make the best of a bad situation. You can join health clubs to swim, play tennis, jog and exercise—all indoors where the air is free of pollution and muggers.

BACK TROUBLES

When I was a young girl, I pulled a muscle in my back while riding. Foolishly, I ignored the pain and got back on my horse. Because I did not realize I had truly injured my back, I developed a trigger point.

A trigger point, in the words of Dr. Hans Kraus, quoted from his book *Backache Stress and Tension*, "can be caused by constant or acute strain of the muscles or by muscle spasm. They are, in a sense, rather like scar tissue of muscles. Trigger points are very painful, and they can literally trigger pain by provoking muscle tension, spasm, or contracture. Trigger points usually appear in your muscles if you let minor episodes of back pain go untreated, and then, once the trigger points have formed, the episodes of pain will increase, both in intensity and frequency."

And I have suffered from my trigger point ever since. During periods of stress and tension, when I get neither sufficient sleep nor appropriate relaxation, my back muscles tense. Tense, they shorten, giving me a spasm. Immediately, I lie down on a firm surface; then after the attack has subsided, I have a therapist massage my back, driving out the pain, relaxing my muscles.

To avoid such problems, you should never ignore any wrench or sprain. If you already are plagued by such a weakness, be sure you get proper exercise, sufficient relaxation, and sleep (check with your doctor). If you suspect damage, see a specialist. Once you can resume normal activities, most specialists will recommend an appropriate exercise program. You will start slowly, careful not to cause additional damage. Eventually, you will be ready for regular exercises, thus ready and able to resist most backaches.

And if you have never suffered a backache, prepare yourself. Someday you might. But if you exercise now, then might will make right. Exercises are the foundation for a preventive program. Thus, if a problem strikes, you will be able to deal with it far better than one who has never exercised. The strongest defense against stress and tension is a strong back and a healthy body.

COMPLAINTS FROM DOWN UNDER: THE STOMACH

Stomachs are not demilitarized zones in the war with stress and tension; they are easy targets.

A bubble of gas is the most common symptom of tension. Worse, and almost as common, is the ulcer: a far more painful manifestation of tension.

Yet stomach tension, too, may be eliminated by a simple

exercise program to strengthen the abdominal muscles.

Without exercise, you will have weak abdominals, a prime cause for lower-back pain. If the abdominals are weak, your lower-back muscles must do extra work and such strain causes fatigue, thus causing further stress and tension.

Remember: A sensible exercise program can even help problems you never thought were affected except by diet.

Stress lands a quick right, a hard left. The stomach muscles tighten, the victim is caught in a ring, battered against the ropes of tension. In fact, the victims have tightened their abdominals, causing cramps. That is no way to brush aside the punches of stress and tension.

With well-exercised abdominals, one may tighten and untighten at will. The result will not be pain, it will be additional strength.

THE STIFF NECK; THE STUFFED SHIRT

If men are required to wear ties, they should not strangle themselves. Instead, they should wear collars a half size too large; and ties need not be knotted like tourniquets.

If one's neck is permitted to function comfortably, one will not only dissipate tension headaches, one may prevent neck spasms, too.

My mother, Bonnie Prudden, wrote: "The muscles of the neck and those which spread upward into the head and downward over the shoulders are prime target areas for tension. Without realizing it, many people tense these muscle areas under any kind of stress." Of course, the result is a pain in the neck and a tension headache.

DON'T FENCE ME IN

Tight clothes generally contribute to tension. A tightly buckled belt is one of the most obvious examples. Another is elastic; clothing, kept in place by elastic may cause pain while restricting circulation.

Standing Tall

Platform shoes and very high heels may cause backache, throw posture out of line, and cause leg muscles considerable pain. Doctors have repeatedly warned against such shoes; but the desire to appear fashionable seems stronger than the desire for physical well-being.

The best shoes are the most ancient: Roman sandals. Of course, they look rather silly with a three-piece suit or an evening gown; but many stores sell shoes designed for feet as well as for fashion.

The Shape of Things to Come

Women need not wear girdles. If women exercise their abdominals, it is possible to develop lithe, elegant muscles, holding in tummies far better than girdles. And girdles are certainly the most constricting undergarments one can wear.

Bras keep pectoral muscles from being stretched. They provide necessary support. Yet shoulder straps may cause back and shoulder pain. Straps should not press down or cut in. They should permit one to move in comfort with ease and grace.

Know Thyself

Love and health begin with oneself. From there, like ripples in a pond, they spread to the entire family. So remember:

1. *Clothes Make the Person.* However, if they are too tight, they can make problems. Loose, comfortable clothing will neither restrict muscles nor hamper the circulation of blood.

2. *Stop the World.* If a situation becomes unbearably tense, then temporarily remove yourself from it. Go for a walk; run around the block; do something to take your mind off it.

3. *The Insulted and the Injured.* Most of us have suffered an indignity here, an embarrassment there. Children are fortu-

nate: they can scream or cry. Yet adults often swallow their insults, without digesting them. Try to express your feelings. With exercise, such tensions can be controlled.

4. *Pride and Prejudice.* Too much may contribute not only to a rigidity of mind, but a rigidity of body, too. And that rigidity causes tension. Again, the answer is exercise.

5. *Laugh Instead of Crying.* William Hazlitt wrote: "Man is the only animal that laughs and weeps, for he is the only animal that is struck by the difference between what things are and what they might have been."

6. *Do Not Take Your Problems to Bed.* They not only cause insomnia, they make lousy lovers. Furthermore, the resulting fatigue is an open invitation to tension. And remember: A firm mattress, without valleys and hills, provides support for a sound sleep and a strong body.

7. *Do Not Eat and Run.* Foxes, raiding a chicken coop, have no choice. And they probably suffer from indigestion. But people deserve more relaxing meals, especially at breakfast.

8. *Exercise.* It's the finest release for the effects of stress, letting tension pour out and disappear. After a hard day's work, you may feel weary; but if you exercise for fifteen minutes, you will feel renewed with energy. The heart rate and circulation will have increased. Formerly tense muscles will be stretched, and the day's tensions will be strangers to the night.

Without tension, without fatigue, one is primed for an exciting evening. Furthermore, at evening's end, one will sleep easily and comfortably.

TENSION

Shoulders and Neck

1. SWIM

Stand with feet apart; bend forward from hips. Swing your arms as if you were doing the crawl. Use a complete circular motion, alternating first left and then right arm. Repeat 16 times.

213

214

215

216

217

218

2. THE BACK OF MY HAND

Stand with feet together or apart, arms at your sides. Bend your right arm at the elbow; now raise it, placing the back of your hand against your right cheek. Now swing your hand away from your face, straightening your arm, swing arm backwards, as if you were doing the backstroke. Repeat the same movement with your left hand and arm. Do series 8 times.

3. THE SHRUG

Stand with feet apart, arms at your sides. Now try to raise your shoulders up to your ears. Now lower shoulders, and lift your head by stretching your neck upwards. Repeat 16 times.

219

220

4. SHOULDERS BACK AND FORTH

Stand with feet apart, hands at your sides. Push your shoulders forward, rounding your back; now stretch your shoulders back, as if you wanted your shoulder blades to touch. Repeat 16 times.

221

222

5. SHOULDER CIRCLE

Stand with feet apart, hands at sides. Push shoulders forward, then lift shoulders to ears, then stretch shoulders back, and finally, lower shoulders. Keep this circular motion going 8 times; then change direction, circling shoulders in a backward motion. Repeat 8 times. Do series 3 times.

6. ARM SWING

Stand with feet apart, arms outstretched at shoulder height. Keeping the hips still, swing your arms from side to side. Let your head follow your arms. Do 16.

223

225

7. HEAD ROLL

Stand with feet apart and hands at sides. Let your head tilt forward (but do not bend the upper body). Now slowly move your head to the right over the right shoulder, back, over the left shoulder, and forward again. Then change direction; roll your head over the left shoulder, back, over the right shoulder, and then rest forward again. Do this 5 times to the right; 5 times to the left.

You can do tension exercises nos. 3, 4, 5, and 7 at any time, any place: sitting at a desk, talking on the phone, driving a car (only do no. 7 when stopped at a red light). Whenever you feel your shoulders and neck tighten, do these exercises; they will alleviate pressure in your body.

8. AIRPLANE STRETCH

Stand with feet apart, fingertips touching in front of chest, and elbows sticking out at sides at shoulder height. Bring your elbows back behind you as far as you can, then return to first position. Now straighten your arms (still keeping them at shoulder height); place your palms up, and stretch your arms back as far as you can. Return to starting position. Repeat series 16 times.

9. PRONE ARM LIFT

Lie prone with your chin on the floor and your arms outstretched in front of you. Now lift your right arm into the air as far as you can, keeping it next to your ear. Chin remains on the floor. Lower your right arm, then lift the left arm in the same manner. Repeat 16 times.

Upper Back

1. ON KNEES, PUSH-UPS

Get on your hands and knees, hands turned in so that fingers of opposite hands point toward each other. Lower your upper body to the floor, placing chin on the floor. Keep your elbows sticking out to the sides of your body and your buttocks sticking up in the air. Now raise yourself. Repeat 16 times.

228

229

230

231

232

2. PUSH A PEBBLE WITH YOUR NOSE

Get on your hands and knees; now stretch your arms out in front of you as far as you can, while resting your buttocks on your heels. Now, as if you were pushing a pebble with your nose, slowly move your torso forward, until your head passes your hands. Your arms will be bent at the elbows as if you were about to do a push-up. Straighten your arms, pushing your shoulders and body upward so that you are on straight arms and bent knees. Now return to original position, and repeat exercise 4 times.

3. PAINT THE WALL

As in no. 1, get on your hands and knees. As if you had a bucket of paint on your left side, and a paintbrush and a wall to paint on your right, reach your right hand under your left side, then swing your arm out and up to the right side. Repeat 4 times and change sides. Repeat series twice.

4. OVERHEAD ARM BOUNCE: SIDE TO SIDE

Stand with feet apart. Raise right arm. Stretch and arc right arm over head and bounce to the left; keep hand flexed as if you wanted to place its palm on the left wall. Bounce 16 times and change arms. Repeat same series 8 times, then 4 times, then 2 times.

5. FORWARD BOUNCE: STANDING, ARMS HANGING DOWN

Stand with feet apart, legs straight, and arms resting at your sides. Letting your arms and hands dangle loosely in front of you, bend forward at the hip and bounce downward as far as you can, without bending your knees. Bounce 8 times forward; 8 times over your right leg; 8 times forward, 8 times over the left leg, and 8 times forward again. Be sure to keep your legs straight.

233

6. PRONE ARM LIFT

Lie prone with your chin on the floor, and your arms outstretched in front of you. Now lift your right arm into the air as far as you can, keeping it next to your ear. Chin remains on the floor. Lower your right arm, then lift the left arm in the same manner. Repeat 16 times.

Lower Back

1. PRONE LEG LIFT

Lie on your stomach, resting your head on folded arms. Keep legs straight and hipbones on the floor. Alternate lifting first one leg (hold 4 seconds), then the other leg (hold 4 seconds). Repeat 12 times.

2. BACK: ARCH AND FLATTEN

Lie supine with knees bent and feet on floor. Keeping your upper back and buttocks on the floor, arch your lower back. Now flatten it, pushing it onto the floor. Hold your back firmly against the floor for 4 seconds and repeat the arch and flattening. Repeat 6 times.

3. BACK FLAT: LEG LOWER

This exercise is essential for lower-back strength.

Lie supine. Bring your knees over chest and then straighten legs so they form a 90-degree angle with your torso. Keeping the small of your back pressed against the floor, slowly lower legs. Lower them ONLY as far as you can WITHOUT your back rising off the floor. (If you feel your back rising, you have lowered your legs too far.) When you reach *your* point, hold 4 seconds, then release by bending your knees over your chest. Repeat 4 times. NEVER lower your legs all the way down to the floor as this will cause back strain. Be sure to go only as far as you can, keeping your back FLAT.

4. DONKEY KICK—KNEE TO NOSE

Get on your hands and knees; keep arms straight. Bring right knee under body, up to touch nose, while lowering head; now kick leg out behind you and lift your head. Repeat 4 times and change legs. Do series twice.

5. THE CAT

Get on your hands and knees; keep your arms straight. Now let your head drop; pull in your stomach and round your back; hold 3 seconds. Now raise your head up and let your back sag; hold 3 seconds. Repeat 8 times.

234

235

6. THE METRONOME

Lie supine. Now raise your legs, bending your knees over your chest. Keep your back flat on the floor. Now lower your bent legs to the left (try to keep both shoulders on the floor). Lift your bent legs off the floor, keeping them bent and your back flat; now lower your legs to the right side. Repeat 16 times.

236

237

Stomach

1. SIT-UPS

Sit on the floor with legs straight, placing feet under something sturdy whenever possible. Place hands behind neck. Slowly lie down to a supine position; then, keeping hands behind neck, sit up. Start with 5 and work your way up to 20, adding a few more each week.

2. GETTING OFF THE RACK

Lie supine with legs outstretched and arms stretched on the floor above your head. Raise your straight right leg into the air; now swing your arms up over your head and bring your body into a sitting position. While doing that, grab your right ankle in both hands. If you

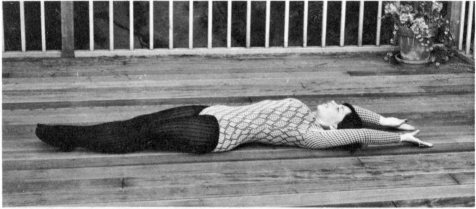

238

239

cannot reach your ankle without bending your knee, grab your calf. Now let go of your leg and lower your body to its original position: legs outstretched on the floor and arms outstretched on the floor above your head. Repeat exercise, raising the left leg. Do series 8 times.

3. ON ELBOWS, BICYCLE

Good for stomach and lower-back muscles.

Sitting on the floor, lean on elbows and forearms. Pretend you are pedaling a bike. As you bring your right knee up to your chest, straighten left leg (but don't rest it on the floor). Now bring your left knee up and straighten the right one. Get a smooth circular motion going. Do 16.

4. ON ELBOWS: KNEES TO CHEST, STRAIGHTEN, AND CIRCLE

This is a very difficult exercise and requires strong stomach muscles. If you are new to exercise, wait a few weeks before adding this one to your daily program.

Lean back on elbows as in No. 3. Bend both knees up to chest. Straighten legs up into the air, then slowly separate them. While lowering them make two half-circles with your legs, bringing them together 4 inches off the floor. Hold 3 seconds and return to the first position, with knees over chest. Repeat exercise 4 times. After several weeks, add 4 more.

5. PELVIC TILT—KNEELING

Kneel with legs slightly apart. Keep shoulders still and buttocks *off* your calves. Keep upper body still and stick your fanny out. Now tuck your fanny under (contracting stomach muscles). Repeat 16 times.

Cramping in Legs

1. KNEE BENDS

Stand with feet together, almost touching, hands outstretched in front of you. Bend your knees as far as you can to a squatting position and then stand straight. Repeat 12 times.

242

241

2. ON ELBOW, LEG LIFT

Lie on your right side, keeping torso off the floor but leaning on right hip and right elbow and forearm. Keep legs straight. Now lift left leg, like half a scissor, up and down, 6 times with toes pointed; 6 times with foot flexed. change sides and repeat exercise. Repeat series 3 times.

3. ON ELBOW, LEG SWING

Lie on your left side, keep torso off the floor but lean on left elbow and forearm, resting right hand in front of you. Keep legs straight. Raise right leg 6 inches above left leg. Now swing right leg forward and backward, like a pendulum, 4 times. Now swing it in a circle twice, like the hands of a clock. Do exercise twice and change sides. Do series 3 times.

243

244

245

4. FORWARD BOUNCE: SITTING

Sit on the floor. Put one sole of your foot against the other sole. Of course your knees will be bent and apart. Grasp ankles and, keeping back straight, rock your torso forward and back 6 times. Now round your back, and pull your head toward your toes and bounce 6 times. Repeat series 4 times.

5. SITTING: KNEES TO FLOOR

This is especially good for stretching the inner-leg muscles.

Sit with the soles of your feet together and knees apart. Place your hands on your ankles, and your elbows on your knees. Push your knees toward the floor with your elbows, as far as you can, then release. (Do not push to the point of pain. Just go as far as your muscles will allow.) Repeat 12 times.

6. ON ELBOWS, BICYCLE

Good for stomach and lower-back muscles.

Sitting on the floor, lean on elbows and forearms. Pretend you are pedaling a bike. As you bring your right knee up to your chest, straighten left leg (but don't rest it on the floor). Now bring your left leg up and straighten the right one. Get a smooth circular motion going. Do 16.

7. SITTING: BENT KNEE, LEG BOUNCES

Sit on the floor, leaning back with arms straight and resting on your hands. Now bend your knees forming a triangle with your legs and the floor. Now place feet apart. Lift your feet off the floor; now put them on the floor. Now bounce them 25 times. If your stomach muscles begin to hurt, stop and continue later on.

247

248

249

250

8. INFINITY LEG SWING

Sit on the floor, lean back on your elbows and forearms. Stretch your legs out in front of you. Lift right leg, flexing its foot. Now turn foot to the left. Cross your right leg over your left leg. Place the right big toe on the floor, on the outer side of your left leg. (If you have to bend your knee a little, do so.) Now twist the right foot, so that the little toe (foot is still flexed) is turned right. Bring your right leg back over the left, placing the right little toe on the floor. Repeat 6 times and change legs.

251

9. SITTING: SIDE TO SIDE BOUNCE—
CHIN TO TOE / EAR TO KNEE

This exercise will not only stretch the backs and insides of your legs, it will help stretch backs and upper hip areas.

a. Sit with legs wide apart and straight. Hold right knee, flex foot to give the backs of your leg muscles and tendons greater stretching, and keep head up. Now push torso forward and back. Try to feel as if you were stretching your chin toward your toes. After 8 bounces, change legs. Remember: Keep your chin up.

b. Sit as in *a*, only this time try to pull your ear to your knee without bending the knee. Bounce 8 times and change legs.

Do series *a* and *b* 3 times.

7

FACE IT

Each morning, I meet my face in the bathroom mirror; each day, my face meets other faces. My face is like a business card; I am aware of how it looks, of what it suggests.

Your face not only suggests, but reveals the condition of your body. Therefore, I can judge the condition of a student's body by his or her face.

If you have a soft, pudgy face, then your body is probably soft and pudgy, too.

If your body does not get adequate rest, your face suffers. A puffy face suggests insufficient sleep, tension, and a dietary deficiency.

Of course, many people are physically fit; yet, they are dissatisfied with their faces. Two choices remain: facial exercises or plastic surgery.

Of course, plastic surgery is not within the scope of this book. Yet I have seen noses thinned, ears flattened to great advantage.

This book deals with exercises. And exercise can suck up a dewlap and fill out hollows, leaving one with a healthy countenance. Not only can exercise do all that; it is obviously far less expensive than plastic surgery.

BEAUTY IS MORE THAN SKIN DEEP

If, as the ancient Romans claimed, art is long and life is short, then you should treat your face like a work of art. Indeed, a face is like a sculpture: it is built from the inside out. Though it contains glands, veins, tissue—it is most like a sculpture in its careful arrangement of muscles and bones.

Exercise can alter facial muscles, especially those controlling a variety of expressions. Your permanent expression should not be a frown; instead, a frown may punctuate a point. And a frown alternated with a grin is an effective facial exercise.

JOWL AND GROWL

When rarely exercised, facial muscles sag or shrink. Exercise regularly, and your face will look strong and firm. Facial exercises are precise, yet simple; effective, yet easy. In fact, making funny faces, in the privacy of one's mirror, will be a pleasant prelude to each day.

FACE EXERCISES

1. HOLLOW YOUR CHEEKS—
RAISE CHEEKBONE AREA

Pucker your lips (as if you were tasting something VERY sour or kissing someone very sweet). Now lift corners of mouth, as if to smile, raising upper cheek muscles. Hold for several seconds, then relax. Do 6 times.

This exercise lifts cheekbone muscles and hollows out lower cheeks; after a few weeks, you will see a change in the shape of your mouth, too. Your lips will begin to curve upward, at the ends, giving you a slight smile.

 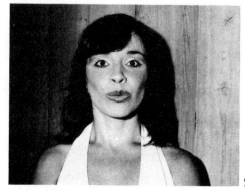

252
253

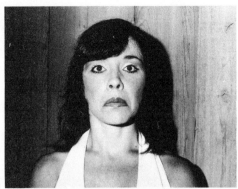

254

255

2. JOWLS

Frown: turn the ends of your mouth down as if you were more than miserable. Now smile, pushing the ends of your lips up. Hold for several seconds, then relax. Do 6 times.

This exercise is good for upper-cheek muscles, and tightens jowls.

3. DOUBLE CHIN

Overweight and poor physical condition are usually evidenced by a double chin. So, first lose weight. Next do the following exercise.

Stick your lower jaw out: lower teeth should stick out farther than upper teeth. Now make a circular motion with your mouth; do an exaggerated chewing motion, rather like a cow. Do it clockwise, then counterclockwise. While you are doing this exercise, lift your head so that neck muscles stretch and tighten. Do 25 chewing circles to the right; 25 to the left.

257

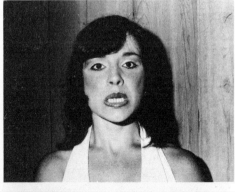

256

259

258

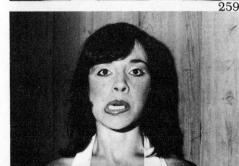

4. UNDER EYES

Close your eyes. Now let your eyeballs move up, but be sure to keep lids down. Do not wrinkle brow. Hold for five seconds and repeat 8 times.

Bags under eyes will become taut, giving one a fresher look.

5. FROWN LINES: THE BLOWFISH

Have you ever seen a Blowfish! Simply blow up your cheeks, filling out the upper and lower-lip area. Hold the Blowfish position 4 seconds, then release. Repeat 12 times.

260

6. LAUGH LINES: THE MONKEY

Try making a Monkey face. Place your tongue on your upper teeth while keeping your mouth shut. Now purse your lips for 2 seconds,

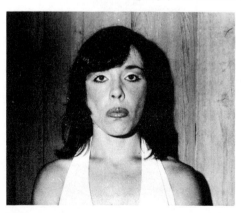

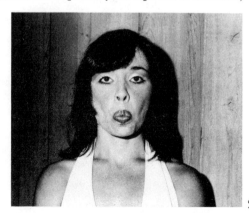

262

261

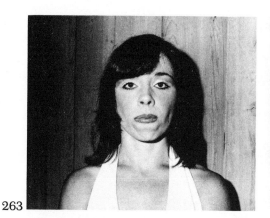

263

then release. Now place your tongue in front of your lower teeth and smile. Hold 2 seconds, then release. Repeat series, 8 times.

264

7. FISH FACE (PULLING IN CHEEKS)

Suck in your cheeks and pull in the ends of your lips. Hold 4 seconds and release. Repeat 6 times. This not only hollows cheeks, it tightens them, too.

265

8

Keep Fit: Look Young

Unfortunately, the moment we are born we begin to age.

Though time cannot be halted, the process of growing old can be slowed. An energetic pace can be maintained, and the dew of youth need not entirely evaporate.

The Inner Sanctum

Aging begins from within. And often our faces and figures reveal crimes we have committed to our insides. I use the word crime because what we do to ourselves, though often unintentional, is criminal.

Indulging in fatty foods encourages arteriosclerosis, and that hampers the flow of blood, not only causing a lack of vitality, but often finally serious heart disease.

While it is true that, as the body matures, the liver is less able to break down alcohol, liquor in moderation is not unhealthful: a moderate amount causes blood vessels to dilate, which reduces the rate at which skin wrinkles. If you have any question about the amount you drink, you should consult a doctor, who can medically evaluate the quantity imbibed.

Paradoxically, if you drink *and* smoke, your blood vessels will remain the same size. Nicotine causes capillaries to constrict, thus hampering circulation, and causing excessively wrinkled skin.

And, as everyone now knows, cigarettes can cause cancer, and some cardiac disease has been linked to smoking.

Gauging Aging

Like anything, if exercise is worth doing, it is worth doing well.

Aging is often an excuse for inactivity; and inactivity not only causes aging, it causes muscles to shrink.

Of course we are less able to perform certain physical activities as we grow older. But performance need not cease, only be gently reduced.

In order to defer a condition of weakness, one must exercise. Yet the exercises must fit the capacities of the person about to exercise. Therefore, I recommend, for all those who have not exercised in years, a consultation with a doctor.

According to an article in *Newsweek,* Dr. Herbert A. de Vries, of the University of Southern California, found that "exercise increased oxygen-carrying capacity—the best single measure of vigor—reduced body fat and nervous tension and improved heart and blood-vessel function as well as arm strength." Dr. de Vries conducted his tests on men between ages 52 and 88.

Not only does exercise reduce quantities of fat, it reduces the possibility of diabetes in elderly people. Obesity in the elderly may cause diabetes as well as heart disease.

Again from *Newsweek:*

"The gerontologists are fascinated with such places as Vilcabremba—as well as with Abkhazia in the Soviet Republic of Georgia, and Hunza in Kashmir, where living well beyond the age of 100 is also commonplace. The diets of the residents of Vilcabremba and Hunza are low in saturated fats—meat and dairy products account for less than 2 percent of the calories consumed—and this, according to current medical opinion, should delay the onset of arteriosclerosis. All three areas are agrarian, and the residents are used to prolonged physical labor."

Well, if you have neither the opportunity for "prolonged physical labor" nor think it much fun, then try exercise. It does not pay a minimum wage, it pays a maximum wage: a long, healthy life.

AGE

1. SIT-UPS—ROLL DOWNS

If you haven't exercised in many years, your muscles will probably not be strong enough to do a regular sit-up.

Instead, start in a sitting position, on the floor. Stretch legs out, placing feet under something sturdy whenever possible. Now place your hands behind your neck and slowly lie down to a supine position. Return to a sitting position, putting your hands on the floor: do not rely, at this point, on your abdominals. When lying down slowly becomes easy, THEN start the regular sit-ups. From the supine position, keeping your hands behind your neck, pull your body to a sitting position. Repeat the roll downs 8 times; repeat the sit-ups 4 times. Increase the sit-ups to 8 times when you are able to.

2. KICKING AWAY THE FLIES

Lie supine, arms at your sides. Now bend your right leg, bringing your right knee over your chest; now straighten the right leg into the

267

air, making it perpendicular to your body. Bend your knee over your chest, again; then return your leg to the floor. Repeat with left leg. Do series 12 times.

3. ARCH AND FLATTEN

Lie supine with knees bent and feet on floor. Keeping your upper back and buttocks on the floor, arch your lower back. Now flatten it, pushing it onto the floor. Hold your back firmly against the floor for 4 seconds and repeat the arch and flattening. Repeat 6 times.

4. PRONE ARM LIFT

Lie prone with your chin on the floor and your arms outstretched in front of you. Now lift your right arm into the air as far as you can, keeping it close to your ear. Chin remains on the floor. Lower your right arm, then lift the left arm in the same manner. Repeat 16 times.

5. PRONE LEG LIFT

Lie prone, resting your head on folded arms. Keeping your hip-bones on the floor, raise the right leg. (Do not bend the knee or let the hipbone off the floor.) Hold leg in the air 2 seconds and then lower it. Raise left leg in the same manner. Repeat 16 times.

268

269

6. SITTING IN A CHAIR

a. *Indecision*

Sit in a chair; rest both feet flat on the floor. Raise your right leg and cross it over your left knee; now uncross it and replace your foot on the floor. Do the same with your left leg. Repeat series, 16 times.

b. *Apple Bobbing*

Sit in a chair, feet resting flat on the floor, about two feet apart. Now bend forward from the hips, bounce your torso up and down, 16 times.

c. *Killing the Bugs*

Sit in a chair, rest feet flat on the floor. Keep back as straight as possible. Now raise right knee up to your chest; hold 4 seconds; then return your foot to the floor. Do the same with your left leg. Repeat 8 times each leg.

270

271

7. ALTERNATE TOE TWIST

Sit on the floor with your legs straight, but spread apart. Your right hand now reaches toward your left foot. Now twist your body, reaching your left hand toward your right foot. Twist again, reaching your right hand toward your left foot. Repeat 16 times.

8. SWIM

Stand with feet apart; bend forward from the hips. Swing your arms as if you were doing the crawl. Use a complete circular motion, alternating first right and then left arm. Repeat 16 times.

9. FORWARD BOUNCE: STANDING, ARMS HANGING DOWN

Stand with feet apart, legs straight, and arms resting at your sides. Letting your arms and hands dangle loosely in front of you, bend forward at the hip and bounce downward as far as you can, without bending your knees. Bounce 8 times forward; 8 times over your right leg; 8 times forward, 8 times over the left leg, and 8 times forward again. Be sure to keep your legs straight.

9

FOR WOMEN ONLY

Being a woman is neither less nor more difficult than being a man. It is different.

Most women are far more conscious of their figures than are most men. (Men frequently complain of overweight wives, but they rarely criticize their own shapes.) Yet, a man with a potbelly is hardly attractive. In fact, his condition is a sign of poor health and can portend a certain inadequacy as a lover.

Not only do men appreciate a beautiful woman, but all women measure themselves by the standards of their most attractive contemporaries. Though such comparisons may end in envy, they should motivate a woman to be as attractive as possible. Competition among women can certainly encourage you to exercise, diet, and look the best you can.

The most attractive women are those with a purpose to their lives. A housewife involved with raising her children and running her home efficiently is a woman who cares about her appearance as well. A working woman (and there are over 30 million of them today in the United States), in a factory, in an office, as an executive, a model, a doctor, or a lawyer, is in a position where her appearance and stamina are absolute necessities.

Housewives have a more difficult time remaining physically fit than working women. Being at home is an open invitation to snack morning, noon, and night. Also, a housewife no longer has to do all her work by herself. She has the assistance of many electrical appliances (not available to her grandmother), and she may have the help of a maid as well. But understand that so much leisure leaves a woman an enormous opportunity to go soft. Such women must exercise regularly and vigorously. If they do not, then their bodies will become soft and plump.

Salad Days

As a teenager, I not only had a sweet tooth, I had an entire mouth of sweet teeth. As I matured, I had found I had to alter my diet if I did not wish to gain weight. I completely eliminated starches; yet sweets remain a secret, though infrequent, pleasure, and remaining thin still requires effort.

Now, my breakfasts are high in protein, low in calories. Periodically, I skip lunch; but when I don't, I eat only a salad. For dinners, either a delicious salad and/or a small piece of meat.

Of course, dieting is only part of the equation; one must add exercise, before a lovely figure appears on the other side of the equal sign.

In my final chapter, I shall not only discuss problems of dieting, I shall provide a number of helpful suggestions, too.

An Hourglass Figure

If your beauty is not to be quickly covered by the sands of time, then you must exercise. In other words, the future is in the present. If you exercise now, you will have a strong, comely body now and in the future. The same applies to dieting: if you want to be thinner tomorrow, then diet today. If you have been overweight for only a year, then you can shed the excess weight easier and faster than one who has been overweight for fifteen years. Fat is like a habit, and habits of a lifetime are difficult to break. But not impossible. As long as you do not accept defeat before the battle has even begun, then you should emerge a victor.

Of course, any woman working toward an hourglass figure wants a flat tummy. A potbelly is, indeed, disheartening. It symbolizes inadequate health and energy. Yet, simply and easily, it can be flattened by a program of dieting and exercising.

She Walks in Beauty: Legs

Most women are not entirely satisfied with the shape of their legs. Some are too thin; others are topped by heavy thighs or end in thick ankles. During winter months, such legs dash about in thigh-high boots, elegant pantsuits, or smart maxiskirts. But when summer comes, legs appear. And many women would like to put their legs in storage along with winter clothing. If you follow my program of exercises, then others may want to follow your legs. Here are some other general ways to help develop them.

1. Walk to work as often as possible. If you use mass transportation, walk to the next bus stop or train station. Climbing stairs is also an excellent leg exercise; it is good for the heart, too. Of course, time and determination decide how much walking you will do. Yet, after a month of regular walking, legs will not only look better, muscles will have been strengthened, elegantly stretched, and shaped; in addition—or by subtraction—fat will have been lost along the way.

2. Either in the morning or in the evening, do the following for *fifteen minutes:* Stand, placing feet together, then rise up on one's toes, now down on one's heels. Do both feet together; then alternate, now left, now right, placing one foot flat on the floor, the other up on its toes. This exercise is particularly effective for heavy legs and thick ankles.

3. Put on some rhythmical music and run in place. Stationary running is superb for building up or slimming down one's legs. There is no loneliness in this kind of long-distance running.

4. If you want to get your family involved, bicycling is perfect. It is not only an effective exercise for legs, it is good for the rest of the figure, too. Pedaling develops lithe and lovely legs; it firms and shapes hips and buttocks; it even slims the waist. In fact, the late Dr. Paul Dudley White has recommended bicycling as an effective defense in the battle against heart disease.

Hip and Beautiful

Hips are often extremely bothersome. Years may glide by; but years of inactivity, poor eating habits, and nervous tension make large deposits in many women's hips. And the interest on those deposits is a fat so hard it seems difficult to remove. But it is not impossible.

Hips respond to a program of exercise, diet, and massage, in that order. If you do my exercises, diet thoughtfully, and massage those hard compacts of fat; then you can reduce the size of your hips.

Stretching the Truth

I have yet to meet a woman who would not like to be more attractive. But such improvement cannot be had for nothing. It requires dedication and work. Gadgets, pills and other magic formulas are plentiful; but only exercise can bring out your underlying beauty.

Of course, every life has its gray days; days when one would prefer to remain in bed. Yet even then you do not have to slip into softness. In fact, stretching is not only a perfect, lazy-day exercise; it is efficacious, morning and evening. It is simple; it is relaxing.

Instead of leaping, like a firewoman, from bed after the alarm has clanged, one should strrrrrreeetch. Reach for the ceiling; point toes at the opposite wall. Deliciously relaxing, a good stretch makes back muscles longer, less rigid. If you stretch arms and legs, feet and hands, your figure will be toned.

And, at night, an uplifting stretch will not only relax muscles, it will help one sleep restfully. And sleep is an essential ingredient for the loveliness of any woman's face.

A Theory of Relativity: Breasts

Breasts have always been important to a woman's self-image. Some women are proud of their breasts; others wish they had more to be proud of.

Just as a nose should fit a woman's face, breasts should fit a woman's body. Small breasts look fine on a small woman; large breasts do not seem excessive on a tall, big-boned woman. Some women want smaller breasts without undergoing the plastic surgery available today; others want larger breasts without attaching themselves to some nutty gadget.

While the size of the mammary gland itself cannot be altered, except by surgery, if one has small breasts and wants breasts to appear larger, the muscles under the breasts may be made larger through exercise.

Pectoral muscles support the breasts; those muscles, when sufficiently developed, are strong and large. They will push out a small breast; they will hold up pendulous ones. (Any woman with pendulous breasts is advised to wear a bra. If a breast pulls too heavily on the muscle, then the muscle will stretch, providing inadequate support.)

If one is too well endowed, the problem may be too much fatty tissue. A simple program of diet and exercise could be all that is necessary.

The following exercises are not just for breasts, for hips, and for legs; they are for the entire woman. And a lovely figure is an excellent reason for being physically fit.

After all, this is an age of unprecedented freedom for women; freedom to be as busy, as happy, and as healthy as we want to be.

Women

1. SWIM

Stand with feet apart; bend forward from the hips. Swing your arms as if you were doing the crawl. Use a complete circular motion, alternating first right and then left arm. Repeat 16 times.

2. HIP WAG

Stand with feet apart and arms slightly raised at your sides. Push your hip to the right, leaning most of your weight on the right leg. Now change direction, pushing your hip to the left and leaning most of your weight on the left leg. (Be sure not to stick your buttocks out.) Keep wagging your hips from right to left, keeping the upper half of your body still. Repeat 20 times.

3. HIP LIFT

For greater movability in pelvic area.

Stand with feet slightly apart and hands at sides. Keep shoulders still. Now lift the right hip up and slightly forward, lifting the right heel and turning the hip inward as if you wanted to see something on the right side of your buttocks. Return to starting position and repeat 4 times. Now do the same with your left hip, repeating 4 times. Do series twice.

4. AIRPLANE STRETCH

Stand with feet apart, fingertips touching in front of chest and elbows sticking out at sides, at shoulder height. Bring your elbows back behind you as far as you can, then return to first position. Now straighten your arms (still keeping them at shoulder height); place your palms up, and stretch your arms back as far as you can. Return to starting position. Repeat series 16 times.

5. OVERHEAD ARM: BOUNCE SIDE TO SIDE

Stand with feet apart. Raise right arm. Stretch and arc right arm over head and bounce to the left; keep hand flexed as if you wanted to place its palm on the left wall. Bounce 16 times and change arms. Repeat same series 8 times, then 4 times, then 2 times.

6. WASHING MACHINE TWIST

Keeping your feet apart, bend your arms in at the elbows and lean forward at the hip. Twist upward from waist, moving side to side as if you were a washing machine agitating. Do 16.

7. FORWARD BOUNCE: STANDING

Stand with feet apart, legs straight, and hands clasped behind you. Bounce forward from the hips as far as you can, without bending your knees. Bring your hands up behind you as you bounce. Bounce 8 times forward; 8 times over your right leg; 8 times forward; 8 times over the left leg, and 8 times forward again. Be sure to keep your legs straight.

8. STANDING: SIDE LEG LIFTS

Stand with feet together, resting right hand on a counter or on the back of a chair for balance. Hold your body upright and keep legs straight, raise left leg to the side as high as you can, then lower it. Repeat 8 times and change sides. Do series twice to begin with; after a few weeks, make it 4 times.

9. KNEE BENDS: SIDE TO SIDE

Stand with feet apart, hands at sides. Bend right knee and lean weight on right leg while keeping left leg straight. Now stand straight and then bend left knee and lean weight on left leg while keeping right leg straight. Repeat 16 times.

10. FORWARD BOUNCE: SITTING

Sit on the floor or grass. Put one sole of your foot against the other sole. Of course your knees will be bent and apart. Grasp ankles and, keeping back straight, rock your torso forward and back 6 times. Now round your back, and pull your head toward your toes and bounce 6 times. Repeat series 4 times.

11. KNEES TO FLOOR

This is especially good for stretching the inner-leg muscles.

Seated with the soles of your feet together and knees apart, place your hands on your ankles, and your elbows on your knees. Push your knees toward the floor with your elbows, as far as you can, then release. (Do not push to the point of pain. Just go as far as your muscles will allow.) Repeat 12 times.

12. SITTING: FORWARD BOUNCE, LEGS STRAIGHT

This exercise is excellent for back stretch and leg flexibility.

On the floor or ground, sit with legs straight in front of you and feet together; toes pointed. Grab calves, and keeping knees straight, bounce forward 8 times. Now flex feet and bounce forward 8 times. Repeat series twice.

13. SITTING: SIDE TO SIDE BOUNCE: CHIN TO TOE / EAR TO KNEE

This exercise will not only stretch the backs and insides of your legs, it will help stretch backs and upper hip areas.

a. Sit with legs wide apart and straight. Hold right knee, flex foot to give the backs of your leg muscles and tendons greater stretching, and keep head up. Now push torso forward and back. Try to feel as if you were reaching your chin toward your toes. After 8 bounces, change legs. Remember: Keep your chin up.

b. Sit as in *a*, only this time try to pull your ear to your knee without bending the knee. Bounce 8 times and change legs.

Do series *a* and *b* 3 times.

14. PRONE ARM LIFT

Lie prone with your chin on the floor or ground, and your arms outstretched in front of you. Now lift your right arm into the air as far as you can, keeping it close to your ear. Chin remains on the floor. Lower your right arm, then lift the left arm in the same manner. Repeat 16 times.

15. PRONE LEG LIFT

Lie prone, resting your head on folded arms. Keeping your hipbones on the floor or ground, raise the right leg. (Do not bend the knee or let the hipbone off the floor.) Hold leg in the air 2 seconds and then lower it. Raise left leg in the same manner. Repeat 16 times.

184

16. ALTERNATE PRONE ARM AND LEG LIFT

Lie prone, with your chin on the floor or ground and your arms outstretched in front of you. Keeping your arm close to your head, as in no. 14, and your hipbones on the floor, as in no. 15, lift the right arm and the straight left leg; hold 2 seconds and return arm and leg to floor. Change sides, lifting the left arm and the straight right leg. Repeat 8 times.

17. ROCKING HORSE—RELEASE

Lie on your stomach; grab your ankles with your hands, lifting your legs and chest off the floor or ground. Go as high as you can; hold 4 seconds, and then slowly lower your body to the floor. Let go of your ankles, lower your legs, and let your arms rest at your sides. Do not bend them. Rest your cheek on the floor, and let your entire body relax. Rest 4 seconds and repeat exercise 4 times. If this hurts, then don't lift yourself too high.

274

18. ARCH AND FLATTEN

Lie supine with knees bent and feet on floor or ground. Keeping your upper back and buttocks on the floor, arch your lower back. Now flatten it, pushing it onto the floor. Hold your back firmly against the floor for 4 seconds and repeat the arch and flattening. Repeat 6 times.

19. BACK FLAT: LEG LOWER

This exercise is essential for lower-back strength.

Lie supine. Bring knees over chest and then straighten legs so they form a 90-degree angle with your torso. Keeping the small of your back pressed against the floor or ground, slowly lower legs. Lower them ONLY as far as you can WITHOUT your back rising off the floor. (If you feel your back rising, you have lowered your legs too far.) When you reach *your* point, hold 4 seconds, then release by bending your knees over your chest. Repeat 4 times. NEVER lower your legs all the way down to the floor as this will cause back strain. Be sure to go only as far as you can, keeping your back FLAT.

20. ON ELBOW: LEG LIFT

Lie on your left side, keeping torso off the floor or ground but leaning on left hip and left elbow and forearm. Keep legs straight. Now lift right leg, like half a scissor, up and down, 6 times. Keep toes pointed. Six times, with foot flexed. Change sides and repeat exercise. Repeat series 3 times.

275

21. ON ELBOW: LEG SWING

Lie on your right side, keep torso off the floor or ground but lean on right elbow and forearm, resting left hand in front of you. Keep legs straight. Raise left leg 6 inches above right leg. Now swing left leg forward and backward, like a pendulum, 4 times. Now swing it in a circle twice, like the hands of a clock. Do exercise twice and change sides. Do series 3 times.

22. ON SIDE: UNDER LEG LIFT

Lie on your left side, resting your head on your left arm which is stretched above your head on the floor. Bend your right leg, placing your right foot behind your left knee. Now, lift your left leg as far as you can, then lower it. Repeat 6 times, turn over, and do the same on your right side. Repeat series 4 times.

276

23. ONE LEG STRETCH

a. Lie on your left side, leaning on your left forearm. Bend left leg at the knee. Bring right leg up and with the right hand grab it by the calf. Now straighten right leg up into the air and pull it toward your shoulder 4 times and release. Repeat 4 times and change sides.

b. After several weeks, as *a* becomes easy, change exercise slightly. Lie on floor as in *a*. Grab the inside of your right foot and straighten right leg. As in *a*, pull leg toward your shoulder. Pull 4 times and release. Repeat 4 times and change sides. Refer to photos 28, 29, 30 and 31.

24. LEGS OVERHEAD: BACK STRETCH

Lie supine. Bring your knees over your chest. Slowly straighten your legs vertically. When your legs are straight, start to lift your buttocks off the floor while lowering your legs over your head. Try to get your feet on the floor or ground above your head, but don't force them. Go as far as you can and hold 4 seconds. Then return to supine position, bending your knees as you lower your legs. Repeat 4 times.

25. ON ELBOWS, BICYCLE

Good for stomach and lower-back strength.

Sitting on the floor or ground, lean on elbows and forearms. Pretend you are pedaling a bike. As you bring your right knee up to your chest, straighten left leg (but don't rest it on the floor). Now bring your left leg up and straighten the right one. Get a smooth circular motion going. Do 16.

26. ON ELBOWS: KNEES TO CHEST, LEGS STRAIGHTEN AND CIRCLE

This is a very difficult exercise and requires strong stomach muscles. If you are new to exercise, wait a few weeks before adding this one to your daily program.

Lean back on elbows as in no. 25. Bend both knees up to chest. Straighten legs up into the air, then slowly separate them. While lowering them make two half-circles with your legs, bringing them together 4 inches off the floor or ground. Hold 3 seconds and return to the first position, with knees over chest. Repeat exercise 4 times. After several weeks, add 4 more.

27. PRONE LEG LIFT OVER BACK TO TOUCH OPPOSITE HAND

This may look impossible, but as you gain in strength and flexibility it is quite simple.

Lie prone with legs straight, feet apart, and hands at sides, about a foot from your body. Lift your right leg and hip off the floor or ground, bend knee, and cross leg over your buttocks, until your toes touch your left hand. Then return to starting position. Now do the same with your left leg, crossing over to touch your right hand. Repeat each leg lift 4 times.

28. PRONE: TIGHTEN—RELEASE

Lie in a prone position, resting your head on folded arms. Tighten your stomach, buttocks, inner-thigh, and vaginal muscles. Hold 4 seconds and release. Repeat 6 times.

10

YOU ARE WHAT YOU EAT

These days, anyone who shops and cooks must know the price of foods as well as their nutritional values.

Nutrition is a comparatively new science, less than two centuries old. And the last fifty years have yielded more knowledge than the previous one hundred and fifty years.

No longer is the apple blamed for the fall of man. Instead, diets rich in calories and cholesterol are leaving people poor in health: degenerative diseases, such as diabetes and arteriosclerosis have been connected to fatty diets.

Yet fats should not be entirely eliminated. Doctors have stated that no more than 30 percent of one's diet should be fat. If one is trying to lose weight, then one must be particularly careful about the quantity and quality of fats consumed. A gram of fat yields 9 calories.

On the other hand, proteins and carbohydrates seem very nearly the champions of health. They are not only valuable to weight loss, they are indispensable to life itself. The dieter should know that 1 gram of protein yields 4 calories. So does 1 gram of carbohydrates.

In this chapter, I shall tell you about proteins, carbohydrates, and fats; I shall provide important information about vitamins and minerals, foods and their preparation, and a basic concept about weight loss.

If we are to survive beyond our middle years, if we are to live in states of health and well-being, then we need to know as much as possible. Knowledge can give us the power to avoid early heart attacks.

You probably know that slim people live longer than obese people. That shouldn't depress you if you are obese; for the *formerly* obese person lives longer than the constantly obese person! The Metropolitan Life Insurance Company has facts to prove it. And I shall give you a few simple rules for losing weight.

Yet, what about those who can't decide if they are overweight? A bathroom scale is hardly an answer, since muscular people weigh more than fat people. Remember: 1 pound of fat can be converted to 5 pounds of muscle; but that muscle occupies much less space than fat. If you have rolls of fat on your stomach, back, thighs, hips, then you are too fat. Most women carry their excess baggage in their thighs and hips—but that is not a curse a woman must suffer forever. And most men wear a spare tire around their waists—that too may be exercised away.

Profession, life-style, and many other variables determine your physique. No one has yet reached perfection. However, some people, such as Olympic runners, may have little or no unnecessary fat deposits on their torsos. Ideally, we would all like to be in that condition; but ideals are only guidelines for directing our efforts. In other words, we must try to keep ourselves in the best physical condition we can. And in order to do that, we must not only exercise, we must eat wisely. We must know what proteins, carbohydrates, and fats really are.

THREE SIGNS OF BEING

Proteins are essential for life, for they not only build muscles, they build a variety of body tissues.

Proteins are composed of the elements carbon, hydrogen, oxygen, and nitrogen, contained in chains of amino-acid molecules. During digestion, a metabolic process, proteins are broken down. Following that, in the small intestine, amino acids are released and carried through the bloodstream to cells. There, they are utilized not only for growth, but for essential repairs, too.

Two varieties of amino acids exist: essential and nonessential. Essential amino acids are not synthesized by the system; therefore, they must be included in one's diet of proteins. The nonessential amino acids can be synthesized by the body when necessary. In other words, you could not live without those essential amino acids provided by protein.

Fish, fowl, beef, milk, eggs, cheese, and nuts yield proteins, ensuring the growth of cells and providing energy.

A well-balanced diet should contain at least 14 per cent protein.

More specifically, doctors have recommended a diet containing about 70 grams or 2½ to 3 ounces of protein each day. Of course, a healthy, growing child requires as much protein as is necessary for healthy development. And most satisfying, well-balanced, and varied diets provide sufficient quantities of protein. In addition, one should make sure that children get lots of milk, especially the non-fat kind.

Carbohydrates are an excellent source for endurance, whereas proteins are primarily building agents. Thus, athletes, engaged in endurance sports, rely more on carbohydrates for energy than they rely on quick-energy sources such as candy. The energy from candy is quickly dissipated; the energy from carbohydrates endures. During digestion, carbohydrates do yield sugar, but not as a chocolate bar would. There are several varieties of sugar; e.g., galactose, glucose, lactose, maltose, and sucrose.

Carbohydrates are found in fruits and vegetables, bread and cereals. Salads are a particularly fine source of carbohydrates. And as I noted with proteins, carbohydrates yield only 4 calories per gram. (Calorie, most simply, means the quantity of heat energy yielded by food.)

The sugars from healthful carbohydrates, i.e., fresh fruits and uncooked vegetables, are infinitely better than those from candy, cookies, and cake. The latter are often prepared in saturated fats; they contain large numbers of calories and provide few nutrients. Saturated fats are a prime cause of cholesterol, leading to the degenerative disease arteriosclerosis.

Fats, too, produce energy, for they yield 9 calories per gram. Yet, calories, not used during activity, are deposited in fat banks, collecting superfluous interest.

Nevertheless, fats remain essential for living. They must be present for vitamins A, D, E, and K to serve their proper functions, after being absorbed into the bloodstream.

Three fatty acids—linoleic, lenoleic, and arachidonic— are essential for health and well-being. One may receive an adequate amount from safflower oil, corn oil, and soybean oil.

In his informative book, *Overweight,* Dr. Jean Mayer, Professor of Nutrition at Harvard University, has written:

"a balanced diet, containing no less than 14 percent of protein, no more than 30 percent of fat (with saturated fats cut down), and the rest carbohydrates (with sucrose—ordinary sugar—cut down to a low level) is still the best diet. It contains all the nutrients needed for life-long nutrition; it does not, through excessively low carbohydrate content, introduce an additional cause of fatigue or irritability; it does not, through excessively high fat content, promote high cholesterol."

THERE ARE FATS AND THERE ARE FATS

Who hasn't heard of saturated and unsaturated fats by now? Basically, these adjectives refer to the molecular structures of fatty substances. Simply, unsaturated fats have fewer hydrogen atoms than saturated fats. Therefore, if you use hydrogenated margarine, you are using a product containing saturated fat.

The fewer the unsaturated fats you eat, the less cholesterol you will consume.

THE FAT DOMINO THEORY

No one seems to like fat; no one wants to be fat. Often, fat people attempt to deceive themselves, believing they are not so fat as they really are.

Fat is not necessarily bad from an extrinsic point of view; it's not bad because a dress designer says so. Rather, fat is intrinsically dangerous because it can shorten one's life.

In addition, obesity may accelerate aging, decrease intellectual performance, and interfere with reproduction. Again, Dr. Jean Mayer, from his book, *Overweight:*

"fat people are more likely to suffer from heart and kidney diseases, high blood pressure, diabetes, and many other afflictions. Surgery is more hazardous when the patient is obese. . . . Excessive adipose tissue also adds to the problem of keeping the whole body oxygenated. Obese people have, accordingly, a diminished exercise tolerance and may show greater difficulty in normal breathing, particularly in the presence of any even mild respiratory infection. . . . Another condition where weight reduction is urgent is hypertension. For there is a significant association between obesity and hypertension."

And if that is not reason enough to be slim, then I shall add one more statement by Dr. Mayer: "Infertility in obese men may be the result of the excessively high temperature of the scrotum because of it being surrounded by folds of adipose tissue." Women may endure menstrual irregularities if they are significantly overweight!

FIGHT FAT. IT'S A LOSING STREAK

Diets for losing weight are not pulled out of a hat by magicians; yet many imply or suggest results that are just short of magical. Such diets abound, and desperate victims go from one to another, never satisfied, never happy.

To lose weight one must follow certain elementary rules. An example will illustrate my point: a busy fireman may burn up 3,500 calories in eight hours. However, a sedentary office worker may burn up only 1,500 calories in the same time. Doing daily chores, a housewife may burn up 1,200 calories. Additional activities may raise her total by another 1,000 calories.

Now, if you consume 3,500 calories, yet burn up only 2,500, then you will surely gain weight. In order to lose weight, one must consume fewer calories than one utilizes. In other words, if one has daily utilized 500 more calories than consumed, slowly, steadily, weight will be lost.

Quick weight loss can be dangerous. Two or three pounds a week is healthier. However, if you are really obese, you can initially lose greater amounts, finally tapering off as the optimum weight is approached.

(I advise all potential dieters to consult a physician before commencing any alteration in their eating patterns.)

Beautiful Losers

You not only want to shed excess fat, you want to keep it off. Through a combined program of exercising, which burns up calories, and dieting, which limits calories, you can maintain an optimum weight.

Habits, daily reinforced, become hard to break. Thus you should develop eating habits that will not permit you to consume more calories than you burn.

The first good habit is to chew and eat slowly. Doing so will give you a feeling of satiety much faster. Not only will you feel full, you will be able to savor the tastes of food—a pleasure the eat-and-run eater does not experience.

Next, meals should be well-balanced and should vary from day to day. If they do not vary, you may overeat out of simple boredom. If meals are well-balanced and varied, one should be able to get all the necessary vitamins. It is better to obtain these essential nutrients from your food than a plethora of vitamin pills; but if you have certain limitations on your diet, or if a doctor decides you need a little extra this or that, then vitamins should be taken.

The Vita Mint

Not only for himself, but for numerous manufacturers, Casimir Funk coined the term vitamin.

As I have already stated, most of us do not need vitamin supplements, for vitamins are present in well-balanced and varied diets. Yet, children may require a vitamin supplement, especially during infancy. Pregnant mothers most definitely need additional vitamins. And, quite often, the aged are provided with vitamin supplements, especially the B-complex.

Following is a list and a description of vitamins. People should not only know which foods contain certain vitamins, they should know the functions of vitamins, too.

Vitamins may be divided into two groups: those soluble in fat (vitamins A, D, E, and K) and those soluble in water (B-complex and C). They all contribute to the normal growth and health of the human body.

THE C-NOTE

Vitamin C, ascorbic acid, is most frequently absorbed from the morning glass of orange juice.

In the last few years, vitamin C has received enormous publicity for its role in allegedly combating the common cold, and people have been buying bottle after bottle of it. However, it is less expensively found in citrus fruits, tomatoes, and uncooked cabbage.

Laboratory animals deprived of vitamin C quickly develop arteriosclerosis. Yet, when sufficient quantities are provided, the condition may be reversed.

No wonder, then, that broken blood vessels, bleeding and sore gums, and fatigue are often prevented by the simple administration of this common vitamin.

One must be sure to receive vitamin C daily, for the body cannot store it. And one should not overcook sources of vitamin C, for cooking often destroys it.

TO B OR NOT TO B

This complex includes B-1, B-2, B-6, and B-12; respectively, they are more formally known as thiamine, riboflavin, pyridoxine, and cyanocobalamin.

B-1 assists in proper digestion, carbohydrate metabolism, and elimination, and is essential for normal growth. It can be found in yeast, wheat germ, whole grains, eggs, liver, soybeans, and nuts.

B-2 serves a variety of purposes. It helps to prevent skin breakage, especially damage to the cornea of the eye. In addition, it assists in the oxidation of cells. An adequate supply of B-2 contributes to healthy-looking skin, bright eyes, and the healthy function of the nervous system. One can get B-2 from leafy greens, liver, eggs, milk, and wheat germ. Though avocados provide B-2, they also come with many calories.

B-6 helps to utilize fats and proteins, helps in the formation of blood. Sources: liver, wheat germ, yeast, nuts, milk, greens.

B-12 is helpful in combating various forms of anemia, for it is essential to the formation of red blood cells. It is found in liver, kidneys, brains, and hearts.

Included in the B-complex are inositol, niacin, folic acid, pantothenic acid, choline, and biotin.

Inositol has been praised for combating deposits of cholesterol as well as helping the body absorb vitamin E. It is found in whole grains, wheat germ, kidneys, liver, yeast, and soybeans.

Niacin contributes to the healthy performance of the nervous system and the liver. Furthermore, it plays a role in the oxidation of starches and sugars. It is found in liver, hearts, kidneys (the variety meats), yeast, wheat germ, leafy greens, and fish.

Folic acid contributes to the formation of red blood cells, and it can be found in yeast, leafy greens, and animal organs.

Pantothenic acid not only plays a part in the digestive process, it is evident in carbohydrate metabolism. It is found in variety meats, yeast, soybeans, and some vegetables (peas and broccoli).

Choline apparently affects the distribution and deposition of fats. It can be found in yeast, wheat germ, some nuts, leafy greens, and liver.

Biotin is supposedly necessary for digestion, particularly of fats. It, too, can be found in liver, yeast, and wheat germ.

E Is for Excellence

Vitamin E, though not yet conclusively examined under close laboratory conditions, is a highly regarded substance; many nutritionists believe vitamin E can be used in treating the heart muscle.

We do know that vitamin E helps the cells to store oxygen. Furthermore, it has a direct influence on animal reproduction.

Wheat germ and wheat-germ oil are fine sources of vitamin E.

The D-fence

Vitamin D has been of great benefit to humanity. Rickets, once a common affliction, was dealt a knockout blow by applications of vitamin D. In addition, this vitamin is necessary for the system's use of calcium and phosphorus. And during pregnancy and lactation, it is extremely important. In particular, children require vitamin D for strong teeth and bones.

Fish-liver oils are an excellent and natural source of vitamin D, as is milk fortified with it.

Of course the sun has been providing a common source of vitamin D. Yet too much exposure, like too much concentrated vitamin D, should be avoided. And if one decides to take it as a supplement, a physician should be consulted.

O Kay

Vitamin K is extremely important for the natural clotting of blood. It is found in leafy greens, particularly raw cabbage and lettuce. Spinach and broccoli are additional and excellent sources for this vitamin.

First but Not Least: A

Vitamin A not only helps to maintain healthy skin, it helps in the healthy function of mucous membranes. It prevents some eye ailments, and it helps children grow into strong adults.

Vitamin A is found in fish-liver oils, beets, milk, tomatoes, carrots, and liver.

Vitamin A has been used with great success to prevent night blindness—look how it helps rabbits sneak around vegetable patches at night!

Strike It Rich: Minerals

Minerals offer assistance in the health of the nervous system, working along with vitamins in a variety of metabolic processes.

Calcium is one of the most widely known minerals, for it is essential to the maintenance of strong teeth and bones. As every mother knows, calcium is found in milk, including powdered non-fat milk, yogurt, and cheeses.

Phosphorus is apparently associated with calcium, for they work together, converting proteins into essential amino acids. Yet, vitamin D must be present for phosphorus and calcium to be absorbed into the body. Phosphorus may be found in fowl, beef, fish, soybeans, and whole grains.

Iron assists in the function of the lungs and is an essential component of hemoglobin. In addition, iron is essential in the diets of women and adolescents, for they have a tendency to suffer from iron-deficiency anemia. Iron may be taken either as a dietary supplement or as a natural ingredient found in liver, eggs, leafy greens, and wheat germ.

Iodine, often available in commercially packaged salt, is important to the proper function of the thyroid. Iodine is available in certain salts, as well as present in fish, especially shellfish.

Other minerals are sodium, potassium, and magnesium. A

well-balanced and varied diet usually provides sufficient quantities of all the above-noted minerals.

A PILLAR OF SALT

Most Americans receive more than an adequate supply of sodium from salt.

Salt is essential for the maintenance of life. And the fluids of the body contain nearly the same proportion of salt as is found in sea water. Thus, a great diminution in one's salt intake is dangerous.

Patients with specific problems are frequently advised by doctors to go on salt-restricted diets. They include those with an excess accumulation of fluid about their hearts; those suffering from high blood pressure; those suffering from kidney disease or liver disease. Only a doctor can determine the correct quantity of salt intake.

However, if one is absorbing too much salt, then one may suffer from excessive water retention. Usually, one needs slightly less than one tablespoon of sodium each day.

If you are one of many women who have complained of water retention, then you have probably resorted to a diuretic. Diuretics should be taken only under the advice of a doctor. Dr. Jean Mayer has written: "Salt restriction is a much sounder and safer measure to prevent excessive water retention during weight reduction than the use of diuretics which, if prolonged, may cause kidney damage."

Many authorities believe water retention is a particular problem of middle-aged women, leading sedentary lives. Others believe that too much salt, causing excessive water retention, contributes to fat, lumpy thighs, hips, and buttocks on women of all ages, both active and inactive.

DRINK AND BE MERRY

Alcohol not only can make you fat, it can reduce sexual and intellectual performance as well. Whereas proteins and carbohydrates each yield 4 calories per gram, alcohol yields 7 calories per gram. A 2 ounce martini yields 160 calories. And a dry wine is no better, for it too yields 160 calories. Sweet wines and the malt in beer are even higher.

I'm not advocating abstinence. I merely believe that moderation adds years to one's happiness, to one's very life.

Cents and Sensibility

Before embarking on the specifics of eating, I should just like to repeat what I stated at the beginning of this chapter. One must not only know the price of food, one must know its nutritional values, too. Exciting and nutritious meals can still be prepared economically.

Born and Bread: Children

Parents tend to feed their children as they feed themselves. Thus, most fat parents have fat children; the parents have not only passed on fat cells, they have passed on fattening habits, too. Even in a family comprised of one fat parent, the child has nearly even chances for being fat, too.

Assuming you and your spouse are healthy and well nourished, what do you provide for your child?

As I noted earlier, vitamin D is of inestimable value, not only for strong bones and teeth, but for proper growth, too. (In Japan, after years of increased milk consumption, children have grown faster and taller than their parents did.) And as vitamin D is present in milk, then milk should be a regular in any child's diet. But serve a non-fat milk, simply to avoid excess cholesterol.

Dr. Jean Mayer has written:

"In fact, outside of vitamin D, healthy children need no special food or special preparation that is not a routine ingredient in the whole family's regular meals, even if the children are engaged in a truly rigorous physical regimen."

And during early infancy, mother's milk is an excellent source of nourishment, passing on important antibodies. In order to lactate properly, a mother must eat a richly nourishing diet: a better than adequate supply of proteins and carbohydrates, yet not too much fat. A plentiful supply of non-fat milk and cheese (especially cottage cheese) could not be better for the lactating mother. And the pregnant woman, too.

Breakfast at Tiffany's: Go Lightly

Start the day with a big breakfast? French toast? Pancakes? Waffles? Eggs? Bacon or sausages? Buttered toast? Cereal? Jams? Sugar in coffee or tea? Atop cereal? Ugh! If you stuff yourself to the gills, then you are going to feel like a beached whale. To keep slim, you should turn out the fats, vote in the leans. In other words, but with the same mouth, one should eat nourishingly, not voraciously.

In our family, we've found it best to avoid highly caloric, high-cholesterol breakfasts eaten by so many Americans; instead, we enjoy a "continental breakfast." This usually consists of coffee or tea, a roll, and either fresh fruit or orange juice. For children, milk is substituted for coffee and tea, and they should be permitted to eat a fully-nourishing breakfast, satisfying their appetites.

Dr. Lawrence E. Lamb has written in *Your Heart and How to Live with It:* ". . . their [Europeans'] daily level of activity is unimpaired and in terms of atherosclerosis they are in far better health than the overweight American." No wonder Europeans suffer less from early heart attacks than do Americans.

In order to provide healthful breakfasts, one must begin by being a meticulous reader of all labels.

The Snack Attack

It often arrives with the suddenness of the attack on Pearl Harbor. And unless one is prepared, the effects of a snack attack can be obliterated only by days of extra-careful eating and proper exercise.

The snack attack usually begins by 10:30 AM. One has an irresistible, but not irreversible, desire for food. Anything!

If one works in an office, an inviting cart is wheeled into tempting proximity. It is piled high with pastries, cakes, and other bad goodies. Beware: It is an invitation, not to satiety, but a fat farm.

Now that Americans have become highly conscious of their health, they should insist that such carts carry fruit, yogurt, and fruit juices. All of those products are quite healthful, require no preparation, and are not fattening.

And if you have coffee, use a non-fat milk. And for either coffee or tea, one should utilize an artificial sweetener. If one drinks large quantities of coffee or tea, then an artificial sweetener may save one from hundreds of calories.

Bridging the Day: Luncheon

Try to rely on salads of either fruits or vegetables, or both. One may include cheese, especially non-fat cottage cheese.

Even if not on a diet, avoid the typical assortment of quickie lunches: hot dogs, french fries, spaghetti, salami, macaroni, liverwurst, bologna, and pressed ham.

In addition, omit butter, hydrogenated margarines, and creams. Margarines prepared from safflower or corn oil are quite good, for they are low in saturated fats.

The After-School Snacking Habit

Though an assortment of cold cuts should be avoided, chicken and even turkey, prepared as cold cuts, are quite good.

They make good after-school snacks, served without bread, but with milk or juice.

The office worker and student have limited opportunities for snacking, but the housewife is vulnerable, for she works in tempting proximity to a refrigerator. Perhaps bored, perhaps irritated, she may take a bit of this, a few morsels of that. While talking on the telephone, she may accompany her conversation with any number of snacks. By day's end, her good intentions have been totally defeated.

Even teenagers, with less time to snack, seem to compress more mouthfuls into a few minutes than do housewives. Scoops of ice cream, boxes of cookies, and soft drinks all seem part of a teenager's life. Certainly, all contribute not only to cholesterol, but to skin blemishes and poorly maintained teeth.

Earlier, I referred to a snack attack, for snacking is insidious. Instead, one should strive for satiety with neither high caloric intake nor high cholesterol content.

Snacking, per se, is not unhealthful; rather it is the quantity and quality of what is eaten. For instance, did you know that 3 ounces of peanuts have about five hundred calories? Nearly enough for an entire meal! Nuts are not only highly caloric, but many of them are a source of saturated fats. One should avoid peanuts, pecans, almonds, and cashews. Even sunflower seeds, now a health-food fad, though safe from saturated fats, are highly caloric.

A wide assortment of fruits and raw vegetables are excellent as snacks. Raw carrots are, of course, an obvious snack; but a more elegant snack might consist of cauliflower and a low-calorie dip.

And, as I noted previously, yogurt is an especially healthful snack. Buy it unflavored, then add whatever fruits or vegetables you like, creating a delicious taste.

A Vast Supper May Lead to a Last Supper

At the close of a working day, one likes to be rewarded with a well-prepared meal. Dinner is not only a satisfying conclusion, it is often a time for a family to gather and talk.

However, before the pleasures of dinner, one must return to the kitchen. More than any other meal, dinner probably requires the greatest amount of preparation.

And, during the preparation, one must be careful to avoid unhealthful ingredients and unnecessary methods of cooking.

If you are frying foods, avoid saturated fats. In fact, one should try to cut down on frying as much as possible, since frying involves more fat than either boiling or broiling. For instance, fried chicken is soaking in fat while cooking.

During the summer months, if you grill over charcoal, you can see fat oozing out of succulent meat and hear the crackle of fat spattering on hot coals.

Salads and Vegetables

One of the best ways to satisfy your carbohydrate needs is with salads and vegetables.

Salads *do* provide *roughage* (especially when uncooked) and fresh fruits too. (I prefer fresh or frozen fruits and vegetables to canned. Fruits picked, then immediately "flash frozen" contain all their original nutrients. With canned vegetables and fruits, one can never determine how long they have been languishing on shelves.)

The Main Course

I have already described the advantages of meat broiled compared to fried. Further, beef contains more calories per ounce than fish or fowl. Yet beef is preferable to pork—for bacon, ham, sausages, and pork chops are extremely rich in fats.

Poultry, with the exception of duck and geese, is not only an excellent source of protein, it is low in fat. And the white meat of chicken and turkey has even less fat than the dark meat from those birds. The skin of chicken and turkey contain fat, but they are unsaturated.

Fish is a superb source of protein, and it is extremely low in calories. Nearly all fish fat is unsaturated. It very nearly sounds like a wonder food!

However, sardines contain comparatively large amounts of fat. And tuna contains even more fat than sardines. If you choose to eat either sardines or tuna, avoid those packed in saturated oils.

Though shrimp, lobster, crab, oysters, and scallops are low in fat and high in protein, they yield much cholesterol. They need not be eliminated from a diet, just served less often.

Lamb should not be eaten too often, for it does contain fat. Fatty lamb chops should be regularly avoided.

Many people baste lamb with a variety of fatty sauces and gravies. Obviously, such coverings are unhealthful and should be avoided.

SANDWICHES

Bread is filling, without being health-fulfilling. If it has really served a purpose, it has made school lunches easy and accessible. But few nourishing ingredients are ever put between two slices of bread; of course, turkey and chicken cold cuts are excellent for sandwiches. Nevertheless, if one intends to prepare, serve, and eat sandwiches, then one should buy bread with the finest ingredients.

DESSERTS

When we were children, our parents might have described dinner as a rainbow; desserts, its pot of gold.

As adults, many of us still look forward to completing dinner with a delicious, sweet dessert. However, in desserts prepared at home, be sure to substitute an artificial sweetener for sugar, to substitute non-fat milk for whole milk, and to substitute unsaturated fats for saturated ones.

If, however, one purchases already prepared desserts, then

read labels meticulously. Buy "dietetic" ice creams, candies, and cookies; they are all tasty and satisfying.

The Menu in Your Life

(A sample for adults wishing to diet.)

BREAKFAST

Fresh fruit and/or fruit juice
One boiled egg
Coffee or tea (use non-fat dry milk or lemon; artificial sweetener instead of sugar)

THE FIRST SNACK ATTACK

Dried fruit, fresh fruit, or fruit juice

THE LUNCH THAT PACKS A PUNCH

Vegetable salad prepared with safflower or corn-oil dressing (with lemon juice or vinegar); or any of the many "dietetic" dressings
OR Low calorie cottage cheese with a small salad of vegetable or fruit
OR Yogurt and fruit
Coffee, tea, or soft drink—all artificially sweetened

THE SECOND SNACK ATTACK

Same as the first. Or, if one's sweet tooth is becoming a pest, calm it down with a "dietetic" dessert.

THE SUPER SUPPER

A large salad; large because it's filling
Mighty Meaty
Fish, fowl, or extremely lean meat; all broiled, baked, or boiled, never fried
If, with meat, you prefer not to have a salad, then cook greens. But, without butter, without hydrogenated margarine, and with little salt.

Instead of bon appétit, I wish you a bon voyage on your journey to health and physical fitness. Happy sailings.

INDEX